C000156497

FAITHFUL GRANDPARENTS

Praise for *Faithful Grandparents*

Faithful Grandparents is aimed at the new or expectant grandparent who has faith but perhaps is looking for a road map of topics that may come up. It is wonderful food for thought in preparation for those important and sometimes difficult conversations about *big* things that come up with a grandchild. It has warmth, authenticity and humility, as well as some really useful ideas about how you might go about talking about moral issues with the generation that in some ways you will have more quality time with than you had with your own children.

Judith Holder, author and TV producer

This book is full of rich wisdom, humour, practical ideas, biblical teaching and cultural understanding. Anita brings some wonderful insights from Old Testament stories and relates them to today's generation. It does not avoid the pain and struggle of being a grandparent but draws on stories from different sources showing us ways to enrich and shape the lives of our grandchildren in creative ways. Anita is inspirational in calling us to pass the baton of faith on to the next generation. We loved this book. It challenged us, made us laugh and stirred our hearts to bless our grandchildren in ways that can have far-reaching consequences.

Canon John Hughes, former rector of St John's Harborne and chaplain to Open Doors, and Annie Hughes, spiritual director and chaplain to Open Doors

I began reading a book about grandparenting and ended realising that Anita had taken me on a journey of the soul. Wise, funny, profound and beautifully written – I pray it will bless each of my grandchildren through the changes it brings in me.

Rob Parsons OBE, founder and chairman, Care for the Family

This book is an eloquent and persuasive call for grandparents to understand and step into the hugely influential role they can play in the lives of their grandchildren. Beautifully written and full of wisdom and self-deprecating humour, *Faithful Grandparents* is essential reading for all current and prospective grandparents desiring to nurture the faith of the newest generation.

Jo Swinney, Director of Church Communications, CPO, and author of *Home: The quest to belong*

Anita's book clearly sets out these challenges of grandparenting against the backdrop of our present culture and, by suggesting that the onus is on us to build those relationships, gives us permission to seek out and explore how best we each might develop lasting, loving links. With lovely examples from seasoned grandparents, scriptural insights and the reminder of the grace of God infused throughout these relationships, Anita offers us a "can do" approach which is as affirming as it is challenging.

Caroline Welby

After more than 30 years working with married couples, we have seen (and experienced for ourselves) some of the challenges grandparents face. Drawing on her own and others' stories and the wisdom of the Bible, Anita helps us to reflect honestly on the journey so far and how we can continue to do this well.

Liz and David Percival, directors of 2-in-2-1

The Bible Reading Fellowship
15 The Chambers, Vineyard
Abingdon OX14 3FE
brf.org.uk

The Bible Reading Fellowship (BRF) is a Registered Charity (233280)

ISBN 978 0 85746 661 7
First published 2019
10 9 8 7 6 5 4 3 2 1 0
All rights reserved

Text © Anita Cleverly 2019
This edition © The Bible Reading Fellowship 2019
Cover image © Getty Images

The author asserts the moral right to be identified as the author of this work

Acknowledgements
Unless otherwise acknowledged, scripture quotations are taken from the Holy
Bible, New International Version (Anglicised edition) copyright © 1979, 1984, 2011
by Biblica. Used by permission of Hodder & Stoughton Publishers, a Hachette UK
company. All rights reserved. 'NIV' is a registered trademark of Biblica. UK trademark
number 1448790.

Scripture quotations marked 'MSG' are taken from *The Message*, copyright © 1993,
1994, 1995, 1996, 2000, 2001, 2002 by Eugene H. Peterson. Used by permission of
NavPress. All rights reserved. Represented by Tyndale House Publishers, Inc.

Scripture quotations marked 'ESV' are taken from the Holy Bible, English Standard
Version, published by HarperCollins Publishers, © 2001 Crossway Bibles, a division of
Good News Publishers. Used by permission. All rights reserved.

Every effort has been made to trace and contact copyright owners for material used
in this resource. We apologise for any inadvertent omissions or errors, and would
ask those concerned to contact us so that full acknowledgement can be made in
the future.

A catalogue record for this book is available from the British Library

Printed and bound by in Great Britain by Clays Ltd, Elcograf S.p.A.

FAITHFUL GRANDPARENTS

Hope and love through the generations

ANITA CLEVERLY

Acknowledgements

It is famously said that it takes a village to raise a child. In literary terms it certainly takes a substantial community to birth a book – the one you hold in your hands contains the wisdom, wit and writing (and editing, which doesn't begin with 'w') of many.

My grateful thanks go to the team at BRF: Mike Parsons for commissioning the book; Felicity Howlett for calming phone calls; Olivia Warburton for kindness and empathy in a difficult season while writing; Rebecca J Hall for overseeing design; and particularly Daniele Och for his patience and complicity in the biggest task of editing. Thank you all.

I'm also very grateful to the St Aldates staff, who have manifested endless patience towards me as I have been preoccupied with grandparents, while leading a church where the vast majority of the community is under 40. Thanks in particular to Simon Ponsonby and Mark Brickman, who read and very helpfully commented on an early manuscript, as well as being tirelessly encouraging. And to our PA Flo Chaffey for printing off numerous copies at the drop of a hat.

My heartfelt thanks also to friends and fellow grandparents who have generously contributed their experience and wisdom, as well as cheering me on at every turn: my prayer partners Judith Stevenson and Joy Potter and their husbands; Clare MacInnes; Richard and Prue Bedwell; Dave and Liz Percival; John and Annie Hughes; Jenny Bailey; Wendy Wilkinson; and Chris Band.

Special thanks to my sister and brother-in-law, Miranda and Peter Harris, who have encouraged me when I was floundering and held my hand all the way through, as well as contributing along with those above.

I'm deeply grateful to Jo Swinney for reading the manuscript and loving it, to Caroline Welby for taking time out of unspeakably full schedules to read and recommend, and to Judith Holder for challenging my prejudices and adjusting my vision. I owe huge thanks to Rob and Di Parsons – to Di for listening to me and believing in me when I wasn't sure I believed in myself; and to Rob for helping me make my voice completely loving and accepting, and giving me serious time and attention out of a life where every minute counts. And I can't exaggerate my thanks to Katharine Hill, my long-time friend, who not only gave me and the manuscript close and careful attention, and helped me refine and craft my writing, but also generously lent me her beautiful seaside cottage to write in from time to time. I am so grateful to you all.

Last, but far from least, my family: thank you to my son, Jack, and to my three daughters, Hannah, Alice and Jemimah, for being amazing mothers to our eight grandchildren – I have learnt, and am learning, so much about being a mother from all of them – and helping us endeavour to be good grandparents to them.

And thank you to my husband, Charlie, a brilliant grandfather! Without your help, patience, creativity, encouragement and love, this book would never have seen the light of day.

There's one more thank you. A lot of this book is about God, and about how as grandparents we might try to represent him and recommend him. In Paul's epistle to the Colossians, he encourages them to be 'overflowing with thankfulness' (Colossians 2:7). I am overflowing with thankfulness to God, because I am certain that through you all, and by his spirit, he has brought this book into being.

Anita Cleverly

For my beloved grandchildren:

'Oh yes! Tell us about Aslan!' said several voices at once;
for once again that strange feeling –
like the first signs of spring, like good news –
had come over them.

Contents

Foreword by Katharine Hill 10

Introduction: The heart of a grandparent 13

1 Twenty-first century grandparents 20

2 Memories of the future 35

3 The art of listening 46

4 This sunrise of wonder...54

5 A grandparent's creed..67

6 Books and the book of books...86

7 Wonderful and terrible: the Bible's grandparents.......................98

8 The body beautiful..110

9 Shifting tectonic plates: culture's changing landscape 122

10 Keeping faith when faith is in question 135

11 A grandparent's prayers...145

12 What about me? Soul-keeping...160

Appendices...177

Notes 182

Select bibliography..192

Foreword

The old saying goes, 'You don't miss what you never had', and in one sense, that was certainly true for me in respect of my grandparents. They died when my parents were young, and I never knew them, so it was only when I had children of my own that I began to understand the vital role that grandparents can play in a child's life.

I have so many memories of seeing my parents sitting on the floor with my children doing jigsaws, making jam tarts, teaching them to sew, collecting autumn leaves, reading bedtime stories and doing a hundred other things besides. In my work at Care for the Family, I have come to see how precious the nature of the grandchild–parent relationship is. As one little girl put it: 'Everyone should have a grandparent, because they are the only grown-ups who have time.' I'm not sure all grandparents would agree with that – life can be just as busy as it ever was – but the relationship can certainly be very special. One psychologist described it as 'an uncomplicated form of love'. Maybe it's because most grandparents can have all the fun of enjoying children's company without bearing the ultimate responsibility for them.

I have had the privilege of knowing Anita as a friend for many years, and, as a wife, mother, speaker and church leader with over 30 years' experience, she could have chosen to write about many things. I am so glad that her passion for her grandchildren has prompted her to write *Faithful Grandparents*. Reading it caused me at times to ache for the grandparents I never knew and gave me a renewed thankfulness for the influence that my children's grandparents have been in their lives. They have taught them patience, kindness and integrity and, perhaps most of all, have shared with our children something of their own journey of faith.

I have been so grateful for that. Research has shown that one of the key elements in passing on faith to the next generation is for parents to have the support of the wider family – especially grandparents – and this truth is the raison d'être for *Faithful Grandparents*. While much of the content is helpful whatever one's personal beliefs, the heart of her book is to encourage Christian grandparents to play their part in passing on their faith, hope and love of Jesus to their grandchildren. Anita puts it like this: 'I dream of one day being able to help my grandchildren grasp the amazing truth that it's possible for men and women to encounter God and become his friend.' She urges us not to take this privilege for granted and to accept the challenge of helping to disciple grandchildren in their young faith. Anita acknowledges that this task is too great for parents and grandparents on their own, which is why she writes powerfully about the part the local church can play – whatever its shape or size – to nurture and guide children in their faith.

It is no surprise to me that Anita has ended the book by speaking about the power of prayer. Prayer undergirds her life, and her example over the years has taught me so much about how we can bring our most heartfelt needs to our heavenly father 24-7 – any time, any place. She gives lots of practical ideas about nurturing children's faith, but emphasises that the greatest thing a grandparent can do for their grandchild is to pray for them – for their character, for their friendships, for wisdom, for protection, but above all that their hearts will be soft and responsive to the love of their Father in heaven.

I love this prayer for grandchildren that she has written using Paul's words in Ephesians 3:

> Father, show them how wide and long and high and deep your love is; show them you care about them more than anyone else does, much more than us or even their parents; show them that your love isn't restrictive, and that you delight in the person you've made them. Show them the immeasurable dimensions of your love, Lord. You can do that!

I don't yet have grandchildren of my own, but if I ever do have that privilege, I want to be a grandmother who prays like that. And I want to be a grandmother like Anita, who laughs and has fun, who spoils with ice cream, treats and too much chocolate. I want to be a grandparent who cuddles, listens and helps build foundations that can last a lifetime. And most of all, I want to be a faithful grandparent, one who does everything I can to 'declare your power to the next generation, your mighty acts to all who are to come' (Psalm 71:18).

I believe this wonderful book will help me do that.

Katharine Hill
UK Director, Care for the Family

Introduction

The heart of a grandparent

All my longings lie open before you, Lord.
PSALM 38:9

We paced up and down, looking out of the window at the garden in its drab winter clothes; looking at each other, each playing our own inner video, and in my case with that nervous knot in my stomach. We hovered by the phone, waiting for the call that would tell us our first grandchild had arrived. Finally, after a long, long wait, with every passing minute adding to the list of possible disasters, the news came. A baby boy had arrived in the world, and we set out to meet him, filled with the heady mixture of fizzing joy and relief. But when we got there, it was to find that the labour had been long and agonisingly difficult, with enough blood lost to necessitate a transfusion, and to see our daughter emptied of strength, pale and in pain. It's impossible to exaggerate the power and passion of feeling that washed over me like a rolling sea as we entered the ward and saw our exhausted firstborn, somehow diminished after her ordeal, and beside her in the hospital bassinet her tiny son, practising sight, as he slowly opened and closed his eyes, and moving his arms in the slow-motion way of newborns.

The initial impact of such an encounter is huge, and for a while everything seemed a whirl, my feelings lurching like a roller coaster from acute anxiety for my daughter to knee-weakening adoration for this tiny boy and back again. But my heart rate slowed with the passing minutes, and after a while I found myself able to stare and stare at Reuben, drinking in the perfect and minute fingers and toes, the scrunched-up facial features, the silky-smooth wrinkles of skin and limb – this whole new person, who had been carefully put together in his mother's womb, as David's marvellous song in Psalm 139 says:

> For you created my inmost being;
>> you knit me together in my mother's womb.
> I praise you because I am fearfully and wonderfully made;
>> your works are wonderful,
>> I know that full well.
> My frame was not hidden from you
>> when I was made in the secret place,
>> when I was woven together in the depths of the earth.
> Your eyes saw my unformed body;
>> all the days ordained for me were written in your book
>> before one of them came to be.
> PSALM 139:13–16

This is a beautiful manifesto for the sanctity of human life – the initial creation (v. 13), the slow and precise process from embryo to foetus. Human life begins at the moment of conception, and there is general consensus that the embryo becomes a foetus, a developing baby, at around the tenth week of development, by which time the brain, heart, lungs, internal organs and limbs will all have formed, as will the sex of the infant, who is now about two inches long. There is such a sense of care and tenderness in the psalm. Knitting and weaving take time and precision, and every stitch and thread counts.

If we stop to consider the biological minutiae of pregnancy, we cannot but say with David, 'I am fearfully and wonderfully made; your works are wonderful' (v. 14). Then he adds, 'I know that full well.' There is something much bigger than itself in this simple phrase, that shines through its five unremarkable words. There's an epiphany here, a revealing to David of the utter miracle of the creation of human life. So David's certainty of God's exact and intimate knowledge of our earthly existence from conception's spark to last breath naturally follows (vv. 15–16). He marvels at the omnipresence of God even in the most secret of places, and praises God for his limitless knowledge of the future.

All of these thoughts tumbled through my mind (in much less orderly fashion!) as I stared at Reuben. What a moment, what a miracle, what a life experience rooted in time and place, yet far beyond and outside both! If you are a parent or grandparent, this sense of miracle resonates with you, for you know it too.

Birth is always a mixture of joy and sorrow, peace and panic, pain and bliss. And this is what families are too. Every human life contains the experiences of triumph and tragedy, celebration and commiseration, and has times of peace and steadiness and times of conflict and turbulence. Every human being is born into a family of some kind, and so every family is visited by the panoply of trial and testing as well as blessing that is given to humankind.

It's into this reality that I hope to speak, with an aspiration to offer some thoughts that may help other grandparents. This is a book about what it means to be a grandparent today. But it is not just about what it might mean to be a grandparent, but also about being one who identifies as a Christian – a disciple of Christ – one who believes that Jesus is the way, the truth and the life, without consigning the vast history of humanity's spiritual quests and discoveries, expressed in all sorts of philosophies and religions, to the not-important or insignificant box. It's a book for people who respect the spiritual explorations of human beings through the ages, yet believe that the incarnation was the most complete revelation of God to humanity, and is the ultimate explanation of who God is.

But who cares what grandparents believe, and why should it matter? Well, this is also a book for grandparents who want to communicate these convictions to their grandchildren, principally through who they are as well as what they may say; through actions and attitudes as well as words. It's a book for people for whom their faith matters, for whom belief in God is non-negotiable. It's a book for people in the second half of life, whose faith has stood the test of time, through tragedy as well as triumph. It's a book that I pray might bring you comfort and strength if you are in a season of testing as you read it.

For some such people it will be a matter of reinforcing and backing up their children, the parents of their grandchildren, who are committed to bringing their children up with a strong faith in Jesus Christ. For others, whose own children do not share this faith, for whatever reason, it will be a question of aspiring to set a good example to their grandchildren and praying for 'conversations that matter' at different times, all the while clearly respecting their own children's opinions and convictions on matters of faith.

And then it's a book for curious grandparents, who wonder what has happened to the world since they were children, who perhaps feel afraid or dismayed by some societal developments, and for whom an explanation that makes sense and offers hope would resonate. I asked many grandparents for their thoughts about such a book and you'll hear their voices from time to time through the pages. Here's one response:

> My request is for a book of hope and reassurance. And a book to help me *not* be an old fogey who goes on about the state of the world and saying things like, 'It's not how I would bring up my children.' I don't want to be a grandmother who is so disapproving that my grandchildren won't come to me because they know I won't understand.
>
> So maybe in the end it's about us and not about the children! How to be an older man or woman today. How to find peace as our families implode and explode. It is happening to us *all*. We are having our lives shaken like never before, and we need to know how to hold on to Jesus.

This is a book, therefore, that will look at the cultural changes that have taken place so rapidly since the childhood of the present generation of grandparents. 'Constant change is here to stay,' goes the saying, so maybe it's also a book for those who at present are parents and therefore may become grandparents in the future, when the world will almost certainly look very different again from how it does today.

I write from the perspective of one who has travelled far and found the hand of Jesus to have proved faithful. He has not let go, even in the dark and desperate times. While I am perplexed and troubled by many things in our beautiful world, my hope is that whether you are reading it as a Christian, an agnostic or an atheist, this book will give you food for thought, and that whatever your convictions you will find in these pages something to nourish you, something to touch you and something to woo your spirit.

While I write chiefly as a grandparent for other grandparents, I pray that our sons and daughters and our grandchildren might also find here food for thought, encouragement for the journey and comfort for the soul.

In Psalm 78, the psalmist speaks of this matter of handing faith in God from one generation to the next:

> Listen, dear friends, to God's truth, bend your ears to what I tell you. I'm chewing on the morsel of a proverb; I'll let you in on the sweet old truths, stories we heard from our fathers, counsel we learned at our mother's knee. We're not keeping this to ourselves, we're passing it along to the next generation – God's fame and fortune, the marvellous things he has done. He planted a witness in Jacob, set his Word firmly in Israel, then commanded our parents to teach it to their children so the next generation would know, and all the generations to come – know the truth and tell the stories so their children can trust in God.[1]

While Eugene Peterson's translation makes comprehension easy, the NIV conveys a real sense of generational descent:

> [God]... established the law in Israel, which he commanded our ancestors [generation 1] to teach their children [generation 2], so the next generation would know them, even the children yet to be born [generation 3], and they in turn would tell their children [generation 4].[2]

For the Christian, faith in Jesus as the Word made flesh and the eternal truth is not understood as something that is subject to alteration or modification by cultural developments, scientific discoveries or philosophical theories. Rather, it is understood as something that is outside time and history, something that is unchangeable and ineradicable and of which the driving force is love.

'Love' is a big word, which can mean many things and has been used to communicate many things, not always easily connected with the generally beneficent meaning of love. For our purposes, it includes peace, patience, joy, sacrifice, suffering, endurance, perseverance, trust and many other qualities that are esteemed in a character.

Writing to his niece from prison shortly before his execution, Dietrich Bonhoeffer addresses her and her husband in the wedding sermon that he was not able to deliver in person:

> Marriage is more than your love for each other. It has a higher dignity and power, for it is God's holy ordinance through which he wills to perpetuate the human race till the end of time. In your love you see only your two selves in the world, but in your marriage you are a link in the chain of the generations, which God causes to come and to pass away to his glory, and calls into his kingdom. In your love you see only the heaven of your happiness, but in marriage you are placed at a post of responsibility towards the world and mankind. Your love is your

own private possession, but marriage is more than something personal – it is a status, an office.[3]

In the same way that Bonhoeffer draws a distinction between the personal relationship of marriage and the public calling conferred by the office or status of marriage, we might draw a distinction between an individual's personal convictions about faith and religion and the permanent or overarching centrality of Christ – his birth, life, death and resurrection – to the Christian faith.

As little as perhaps 20 years ago, that paragraph would not possess the inflammatory potential that it does today! In the new era of post-truth and the more jaded era of relativism, the suggestion that there are permanent truths, such as those expressed in Psalm 78, can be greeted with anything from cynicism or pity to outrage. I hope such a suggestion will not prompt such a reaction in you, but rather pique your interest and draw you into thoughts more inspired than inflammatory, more consoling than contentious.

When researching material for the book, I was sent a blog post entitled 'Gifts grandparents give'.[4] The writer listed celebration, companionship, community and character as these gifts, and summed up her thoughts like this: 'Grandparents recognise and call out the good, offering us roots while honouring our wings.' Poetic, true – and aspirational!

We'll be taking a closer look at all the aspects of being a grandparent that are highlighted here. All of them reflect the longing that is at the heart of this book. Please come with me to think about being faithful grandparents, keeping faith alive against increasing odds and being committed to communicating it in a myriad of ways as we pray and long for its safe passage from one generation to the next.

1

Twenty-first century grandparents

Even when I am old and grey, do not forsake me, my God, till I declare your power to the next generation, your mighty acts to all who are to come.

PSALM 71:18

I am where I am today because my grandmother gave me the foundation for success.

Oprah Winfrey[1]

Quite late in his life, my father undertook an imaginative and touching project. He interviewed my mother at some length about her unusual childhood, and made a CD recording of their conversation. He did this for posterity, and he did it with heart-breaking love, asking his questions with great tenderness and patience. He died eight years before my mother and not until two years after her death could I bring myself to listen to voices I loved but could no longer hear.

The conversation between my parents was in a way a study of grandparents, which is a rare thing. The last thorough study of grandparenting was conducted over 50 years ago, in 1965. University of Chicago's Bernice Neugarten, one of the leading gerontologists at the time, identified five patterns of grandparenting.[2] I wonder whether you can relate your grandparents or yourself to one of these:

1 Formal: follows what are believed to be the appropriate guidelines for the grandparenting role, which include providing occasional services and maintaining an interest in the grandchild, but not becoming overly involved.
2 Fun-seeker: emphasises the leisure aspects of the role and primarily provides entertainment for the grandchild.
3 Surrogate parent: takes over the caretaking role with the child.
4 Reservoir of family wisdom (usually a grandfather): the head of the family who dispenses advice and resources but also controls the parent generation.
5 Distant figure: has infrequent contact with the grandchildren, appearing only on holidays and special occasions.

My own grandparents fell into the fifth category – distant figures with whom we had infrequent contact and who we saw only on holiday visits and special occasions. This was not for any relational reason, but simply because of geography. My parents were both born and brought up in the Republic of Ireland and moved to England after their marriage so that my father could take up a teaching post at an English public school, where he taught classics and later became a housemaster. Typical of her time, my mother abandoned her training as an occupational therapist to marry my father. Both had previously been in the army.

As a consequence, my grandparents were mysterious and fascinating, especially my maternal grandmother, who had married a man 27 years her senior (who died in the year I was born.) Theirs was an unconventional marriage, according to my mother, although it was typical of the time in its remoteness and formality. They lived on a farm, where my grandmother bred smooth-haired fox terriers and Dobermanns, which she showed at Crufts and elsewhere for many years. It was perhaps this aspect of her life that accounted for her elegant and flamboyant dress sense.

My paternal grandmother was altogether different: small and very cosy, not at all fashion-conscious, and perpetually buying and giving presents. Her husband, my grandfather, was tall and thin, with a serious face, and worked for the pharmaceutical company Allen and Hanbury, as well as having enlisted in the army and fought in both wars. I found them both fascinating, intriguing and somehow exotic, as a child might, but in those pre-internet days, distance took its toll, and I hardly knew them at all. Even their deaths didn't make much of an impact. Away in France, at the age of 17, I received from my host family's mother a blunt announcement one day, with no warning at all: '*Votre grand-mère est morte.*'[3] I think I was more upset by the woman's total absence of emotional intelligence than by the loss of my grandmother.

As well as recording the long conversation with my mother, my father had the wisdom to write a sort of family history for his children and grandchildren, in which he paints a portrait of these figures who are so dimly lit for me. He writes of my mother's father:

> [He] was what was called in those days a gentleman farmer. On [my mother's] birth certificate it just says 'Gentleman'! He was born in 1866. In his prime he was a fine figure of a man, a person of strong principles and character. In the years before World War I, he looked after the three family farms, going about a good deal on horseback. He was a well-known rider, nicknamed 'Brave Dean'. Being a gentleman farmer did not mean being rich. The land on which you farmed – mostly fattening livestock for the market – had its value, but the income to be had from it was uncertain, and the lifestyle was plain and simple.

> During the first war he served in the Army Service Corps, becoming a captain, and travelling overseas to Thessalonica. Soon after the end of the war, he, now 46, married your 19-year-old grandmother. With a clutch of contemporary, fashionable names – Winifred Lorna Gwendoline – she was always known as Johnnie (and much later to us as Granjohn) possibly because she was a true tomboy, or maybe because her

parents had hoped for a boy. She learnt to ride and shoot as well as any boy, and for the last two years of the war was in London serving the war effort by driving and maintaining quite heavy delivery lorries with massive engines and solid tyres. However, she also enjoyed dinners and theatre trips with a series of admiring young men!

My mother went to the village school for a short time, but after the family moved to the farm, she never went to school again. Her older cousin, who was an intellectual and literary woman with an honours degree from Trinity College in Dublin, used to ride out from Slane on her bicycle five days a week, and teach my mother and her brother 'all that anyone needs to know about reading, writing and arithmetic, plus a love of English literature and a great respect for beauty and truth'.

All of this describes my mother's unusual childhood. My grandmother was, I think, far more interested in her dogs than in her children, and as result my mother's affections were more readily given to Lizzie the housekeeper, who almost certainly offered 'Miss Betty' more maternal care than my grandmother did.

This exotic, eccentric woman was my last surviving grandparent. In her late 70s, she moved from Ireland to west Wales to live near my parents, themselves nearing retirement. Myself now an adult, I was therefore able at this late stage to get to know this feisty, fascinating woman a little.

I cleaned house for her for a while, and eventually discovered that she would place a little pile of cigarette ash under a table to see how thorough my cleaning was. She often smoked two cigarettes at the same time, holding one in each hand, which was a source of anxiety for my parents. And she had a fascinating turn of phrase, always delivered in the Irish lilt that I adored, and still do: 'Ach, the traffic in this village goes so fast it takes the sight out of your eyes.'

Invited to supper at my parents' house, she asked my father what she should wear. 'Oh, nothing,' he replied. 'It's just a simple supper.' She duly turned up and flung open her coat to reveal just underwear! 'Well, you said I was to wear nothing,' she explained.

Towards the end of her life, when she was in hospital with a broken hip, I went to visit her with my new husband. Trying to be thoughtful, I suggested he wait downstairs while I scout out the lie of the land. 'Where the hell is Charlie?' came her voice from the far corner of the ward. 'I haven't seen the sight of a decent man for weeks.' This was a woman who even in her 80s was an ardent fan of boxing on the TV, claiming to love the bodies of the men she watched fighting, just as she loved watching bare-chested builders working on her house or other houses in the village.

My mother could not have been more different from her – a shy, reserved woman, who perhaps because of her lack of education (though the education she received from cousin Emma was better than many) lacked confidence and was not at all outspoken like her mother, though her quiet temperament was almost certainly a response in part to her mother's extroverted nature.

The story of my grandparents, and in particular my maternal grandmother, is a reminder that, while grandparents may be relegated to the past and regarded as sweet but irrelevant, every individual is completely unique, with their own fascinating history. It's a no-brainer – getting to know your grandparents opens up a whole new world, another time, another place. I wish I'd had a chance with the rest of mine.

Who are we as grandparents? One thing to note is that we have a rich, diverse and complex genetic history. Every sexually reproducing person has a maximum of four genetic grandparents, eight genetic great-grandparents, 16 genetic great-great-grandparents, 32 genetic great-great-great-grandparents, 64 genetic great-great-great-great-grandparents, and so on. Each of us is a refined composite of a whole host of genetic individualities. While we and our children have added to the rich tapestry of our grandchildren's genes, we mustn't forget that our own tapestry is equally marvellous, stretching back through the generations as it does. We're not like iPhones, each version adding improvements to the basic first model.

Grandparents are a rich source of learning about the past, a lot more interesting than a school textbook. In addition, we're quite likely to relate more easily to our grandparents, given the normal separating tensions that occur between children and parents.

With the role of grandparents rapidly evolving, more study is now taking place, mostly in the United States, but also in Europe. Three of the different 'types' of grandparent identified by Neugarten – 'formal', 'reservoir of family wisdom' and 'distant figure' – provide an immediate contrast with today's generally much more involved grandparent. What were believed to be the appropriate guidelines, as seen in the 'formal' type (to be polite but remote) and the 'reservoir of family wisdom' type (characterised by control), are both becoming much less common, thankfully in the latter case.

Here are some current definitions of contemporary grandparenting, with a touch of humour, which highlight the contrast:

Grandparent: one who breaks most of the rules and loves every second of it.

Grandparents: parents, but with more sleep, fewer rules and an endless supply of sweets.

Grandparents: so easy to operate, even a child can do it.

So different from the grandparents I never got to know well. No one would deny that becoming a parent is a defining moment in a person's life – many people describe the birth of their first child as one of the most momentous events of their life – but becoming a grandparent is also a rite of passage and is often a profound and emotional experience. Gransnet, and other similar internet sites, are full of little sayings (albeit often sentimental) that try to express this, such as, 'Just when I thought I was too old to fall in love again I became a grandparent.'

Being a grandparent is more complicated than being a parent, because we don't choose to become one; someone else chooses for us. Lots of emotions accompany becoming a grandparent – pleasure, tension, anxiety, gratitude and for some there's even a bit of resentment, as they are moved away from the centre of the relational circle. The new arrival brings positive and negative expectations for the grandparent, both of themselves and their adult children. At the same time, many grandparents experience a love almost as overwhelming as they felt when their own child was born.

Grandparenting is just what it says: grand. The dictionary definition of 'grand' is 'magnificent, splendid, noble, wonderful or very pleasing; of great importance and distinction'. Who wouldn't want such a title? Yet the title 'grandparent' seems less grand than that of 'parent', perhaps because it's often seen as synonymous with old, which is considered bad in our youth-obsessed, age-rejecting culture.

But grandparenting today is not necessarily about old age; many healthy, active, working baby boomers are becoming energetic grandparents. TV and children's books often portray grandparents as fussy, aged and sedentary, perhaps with infirmities (Roald Dahl, guilty as charged for your portrayals of irascible, unpredictable grandparents!), but many children today have grandparents aged between 40 and 60. The typical screen grandparent should really be a great-grandparent. The woman who has infant grandchildren is not likely to have silver hair in a bun, but would be portrayed more realistically in jogging clothes on her way to the gym or in a suit coming home from work.

It hasn't always been like this. The role and influence of grandparents have changed beyond imagination, and generally for the better, over the centuries. Here's a brief overview of some of the changes.

During the 18th and early 19th centuries grandparents, especially grandfathers, exerted considerable economic and social influence based on land ownership. Older male landowners generally retained both their land and their authority over their families until they died.

With the industrial revolution, however, this authority and control diminished as new technology made the talents of the old seem obsolete, and the new economy provided an attractive alternative to following the family business. As life expectancy increased, so did the number of tri-generational households, with the elderly increasingly requiring care. Yet it was the elderly and infirm who traditionally held authority, so the evolving situation naturally led to conflict and dissention in families, with younger generations ready to assume leadership and take the initiative.

In 1885 Samuel Butler wrote:

> I believe that more unhappiness comes from this source [tri-generational households] than from any other. I mean from the attempt to prolong the family connection unduly and make people hang together artificially who would never naturally do so... and the old people do not really like it so much better than the young.[4]

The view of old people as burdensome and unproductive slowly emerged, stemming from the growth of tri-generational households. Ageing was viewed almost as a disease, leading to older people being less valued, especially as workers, and sometimes also within the family.

As a consequence, households started to include two rather than three generations. In 1900 over 60% of older adults lived with adult children; by 1962 it was 25%, and by 1975 only 14% cohabited with adult children. By now older adults had started seeing autonomy and leisure as the goals of the 'golden years'. Grandparents no longer had an important economic role in family life, but nor did they now pose any threat. Mutual independence meant they could become friends with their grandchildren. While it's still true that many children are encouraged to be polite to their grandparents, the onus is on the grandparents to invest their energies in making friends with their grandchildren, rather than waiting to be venerated. They have travelled a long way from being in charge of the family to having to build their own role in the family. This isn't a bad thing; it's a real – and good – example of giving without counting the cost.

The dramatic increase in longer and healthier life expectancy has steadily produced a society in which many of us can expect to become great-grandparents as well as grandparents. This is true across the social spectrum. A minister friend remembers the presence of great-grandparents in his congregation, each generation of girls becoming pregnant in their teens. At the other end of the childbearing spectrum, with children sometimes, if rarely, being born to mothers in their 50s, and many now delaying childbearing until their 30s or 40s, there are some who become parents at the age previous generations were grandparents.

Grandparenting has also become more difficult to define than it was in earlier times, and the baby boomer generation (to which I belong) is changing both grandparenting and the concept of ageing in general. Those born in the years immediately after World War II grew up in a time of radical social change and taboo-breaking, and they still are an outspoken, rather than quiet and acquiescent, generation. As the family changes, grandparenting changes, and it's becoming a much more complicated picture to paint. Lots of factors contribute to this.

First, hugely increased mobility means that families are often spread out geographically, so lots of children aren't able to see their grandparents regularly. This can sometimes lead to a lack of interest in the lives of grandparents, so that grandchildren may grow up without any sense of their family history or of the now-distant youth of their grandparents.

Second, the pace of life has quickened exponentially, as electronic communications have taken centre stage in our lives. This means that even families who live near one another may not be able to, or may choose not to, spend so much time together as was natural for former generations.

Third, declining fertility rates and rising life expectancy mean that families today are often shaped like a beanpole, with a more equal number of people in each generation, rather than a pyramid, as used to be the case, with a few older members at the top and lots of young members at the bottom. This is further accentuated by people choosing to have fewer children, a choice often influenced by pursuing a career before having children at a later age.

With fewer family members in the clan, it becomes more important to maintain intergenerational relationships if family contact and coherence is not to be lost:

> Contact with grandchildren generally declines as grandchildren reach adulthood and embark on their own independent life – unless proactive steps are taken by the grandparents to counteract diminishing contact.[5]

One thing that will help us in this is to understand as much as we can of the different things that being a grandparent might mean today. Consider the huge diversity of situations that a grandmother might find herself in today:

- A woman holds a full-time managerial position in a multinational company, and on the weekends also makes it a priority to spend at least a couple of hours visiting her four-year-old granddaughter.

- A 52-year-old housewife can hardly wait for her twin grandchildren to be born.
- A 43-year-old divorced woman goes to the hospital to see her first grandchild.
- A 62-year-old grandmother helps her teenage granddaughter through the divorce of her parents.
- An immigrant grandmother, living with her daughter and son-in-law, participates in child-rearing and passes down traditions from the 'old country'.
- Another grandmother helps her teenage daughter care for her new baby as they all share a home.
- A woman and her husband, hoping to retire, must now continue working, as they are raising their grandson because his mother is addicted to drugs.
- A couple goes to court to try to get visiting access to their three young grandchildren, because the parents are denying them access.
- A remarried woman buys Christmas presents for her three biological grandchildren and two step-grandchildren.
- A son brings his mother to live with him, his wife and two teenagers after she is diagnosed with Alzheimer's.

This is just a handful of examples, by no means exhaustive, among which we note that grandparenting brings sadness as well as joy. A number of the examples above reflect the pain and suffering that is part of being human, and one of the most troubling is that of a couple going to court to gain visiting access to their grandchildren, something that has become increasingly common. Some 2,000 grandparents applied for child-arrangement orders in 2016, an arduous and very costly process. Even if the court rules for access, there is little that holds the parents to abide by the court ruling. And who among us wants to access our grandchildren via the law?

When access to grandchildren is blocked, it can feel like what some grandparents call a 'living bereavement'. It can have very negative effects on physical as well as emotional health. Studies show that:

Grandparents who are unable to maintain contact with their grandchildren due to parental divorce or disagreements within the family are likely to suffer a variety of ill consequences, including poor mental and physical health, depression, feelings of grief, and poorer quality of life.[6]

Tragically, there are even stories of grandparents sending gifts and cards for birthdays, only to receive a visit from the police investigating an accusation of harassment.

The good news is that in 2018 the Ministry of Justice in the UK began to examine proposals for giving grandparents an automatic right to see their grandchildren. MPs from all parties in the UK are backing an amendment to the Children's Act of 1989 to enshrine in law the child's right to have a relationship with their grandparents and other close members of their extended family.

As journalist Allison Pearson wrote:

To say this reform is long overdue is putting it mildly. The law has failed quite abysmally to keep pace with social changes which have seen grandparents assuming an ever-greater role in youngsters' lives… Two-thirds of the nation's grandparents – that's five million people – now provide regular childcare for their grandchildren.

She goes on to say that many women feel confident about going back to work because 'not only is granny cheaper than childcare, but she's one of the few people who loves your child as much as you do… This vast unpaid contribution to the well-being of society is scandalously unacknowledged.'[7]

Anne Longfield, the Children's Commissioner for England, is behind the push for reform. Speaking specially, but not exclusively, of children from broken homes, she says, 'Children should have the right to keep in touch with their grandparents.' She is anxious about the fact that there is now a whole generation of parents who deal with behaviour management through 'super-nanny' instruction, from websites or TV, and she's keen to see parenting, including sex education, put back in the hands of parents:

> If you go back a couple of generations you would have family members who would live in the same town, the same street, the same house... You would gain information because you would have your own mum on hand... I grew up in a household with grandparents – I know how it anchors you in life, and the benefits it can bring.[8]

For some, the grandparent season can be a second chance. Grandchildren can offer a fresh start. Maybe we feel that we didn't spend as much time with our children when they were young as we would have liked, perhaps because of work demands or what we now see as missed opportunities. We learn from the mistakes we made in our parenting days from the new batch of little ones – hindsight is a beautiful thing! Grandparenting offers many of the joys and benefits of parenting, without many of the hassles, constraints and day-to-day responsibilities.

Apart from all this, the grandparent–grandchild relationship is second in emotional importance only to the parent–child relationship. One of the goals of this book is to bring hope and encouragement to grandparents that, whatever our unique context, we can enjoy loving and being loved by our grandchildren, and that there can be close and valued relationships between grandparents and their grandchildren. In one survey, many respondents said they wished they could see their grandchildren more often. And one of the most popular answers to the question 'What is most satisfying about being a grandparent?' was 'Passing on family and religious values'.[9] As Christian grandparents, we want somehow to convey not so much religious values, as the joys of knowing the fatherhood of God, the friendship of Jesus and the help of the Holy Spirit, and to be a good ambassador for the truths all these embody.

Grandparents generally receive a good press today, certainly when compared with the results of case studies from the 1930s to the 1950s,[10] which reflected the interfering and didactic ways of past generations, when grandmothers were often stricter and more authoritarian than mothers. Both my mother and mother-in-law (both born in the 1920s) describe their grandmothers as stern and frightening:

> My maternal grandmother was rather wealthy – she had a chauffeur, and she was a bit frightening. My paternal grandmother lived with us, and I didn't like her because my mother didn't like her. I suppose I just copied my mother.[11]

> My grandmother was a very old lady, looked after by my maiden aunt Kathleen, herself a rather fearsome figure to a child. I didn't really like visiting her, because we had to go up to the bedroom where she resided in bed, with a fire in the room... We were taken up to the bedside and I suppose we were kissed. It was all rather horrible, really. She had black on, with a black ribbon round her neck and a cap. I think it only happened once a year.[12]

While writing this chapter, a newspaper article caught my eye: 'Evolution dictates you tell us a story, Gran!' The article reported that 20 years of research by American anthropologists among a remote Amazonian tribe of Amerindian people in Bolivia suggests that time with Granny and Grandpa is not just about family bonding, but that grandparents may have evolved specifically to pass on information to younger generations. This, it said, could help answer the much-studied question of why humans live longer than most other primates. Most primates rarely live beyond their 50s, while women often survive for decades after the menopause. The research discovered that with fading strength and productivity came increasingly powerful storytelling. While parents in the tribe provide day-to-day instruction, the grandparents provide the bigger picture, transmitting history and culture. Of the younger members of the tribe, 84% said they heard most of their stories from older relatives, mostly grandparents.[13]

In the light of this, we have so much to offer our grandchildren, because in a way this book is all about providing the bigger picture. So come with me and we'll explore what we expect of ourselves as 21st-century multipurpose and multifunctional grandparents. I want to hold out encouragement to grandparents who, often with a deep longing, desire to communicate their faith and their conviction that knowing God is a wonderful thing.

We've seen that if we want to be close to our grandchildren, we need to take proactive steps to plant, water and tend our precious friendships with them right from their earliest days, if we can. Let's look at the many and diverse ways grandparents can connect and love without being intrusive or seeming bossy.

But just a word to you if you're reading this and thinking, 'I've missed the boat; it's too late.' In the upside-down (or right-side-up) economy of the kingdom of God, the last shall be first and the first shall be last. With God, it's never too late to start again or to start something new, and it's my prayer that if you're reading this from a place of loss or family suffering, you'll find great hope for the days ahead as we travel on together.

2

Memories of the future

Then Naomi took the child in her arms and cared for him. The women living there said, 'Naomi has a son!'
RUTH 4:16–17

It is one of nature's ways that we often feel closer to distant generations than to the generation immediately preceding us.
Igor Stravinsky[1]

On a visit to her daughter's family, Rebecca told her granddaughter Jessica that the following evening she'd be staying with Grandpa's mum, who lived nearby. 'Why aren't you staying with us, Granny?' asked Jessica. 'Because Great-granny-round-the-corner won't be here forever, so I want to share myself out between you and her,' Rebecca replied. The next day the whole family, including Great-granny-round-the-corner, convened at a pub for Sunday lunch. Jessica sprang from the car, bounded straight up to her great-grandmother and announced with a flourish, 'Granny says you're gonna die soon.' Fortunately, Great-granny was possessed of good humour. 'Really?' she said with a smile.

* * *

Arriving at the wedding in her finery, Eleanor hugged her grand-children, so happy to see them. She found herself a little tense during the service as Freddy crawled along under a row of seats, having spotted an iPad that the parents of another small boy had had the wisdom to bring. Would there be a battle of wills over who should hold it? (Freddy, she knew, would ignore the concept of ownership.) Would his foot catch in someone's gorgeous wedding garb? But the service came to an end without drama, and only moderate disruption, and Eleanor's shoulders relaxed as the celebration got under way and the children roared off round the church. Suddenly, she was aware of Clara at her elbow. 'Granny, I like your dress. Can I have it when you die?' Clara asked. 'I very much hope you can have it long before I die,' replied Eleanor, as Clara vanished into the crowd again.

* * *

Looking after her grandchildren while her daughter and son-in-law were away, Helen arrived at school to pick up nine-year-old Angus and immediately realised he was very upset. His shoulders were hunched, and his hood covered much of his face. 'Come on, darling, let's go home, then you can tell me what's happened,' said Helen gently, putting her arm round Angus, who was shrinking into himself. Safely back home, with comforting biscuits and squash, his tear-stained cheeks now visible, Angus explained what the matter was. The class trip was coming up, and everyone had been asked to write down who they'd like to share a room with. Angus wanted to share with his best friend Dan, but found out that Dan had bowed to peer pressure (and the random meanness of children) and obeyed the instruction to choose Tommy instead of Angus.

'Granny, do you think I could text Mum?' asked Angus. 'Of course, darling,' replied Helen. 'Here's my phone; let me find Mum's number.' Silence fell as Angus concentrated on his message. Helen sipped her tea, her heart strings pulled by this pain she could only watch, but not take away.

Angus frowned, pausing in the focused task of texting. Suddenly, he looked up and said, 'Granny, how do you spell f---ing?' For a split second, Helen wondered if she might faint from shock, but she took a deep breath, took the phone and saw the message so far: 'Dear Mum, Dan is a fu–'. I wonder what you think she did? She wisely took another deep breath, handed back the phone and dictated the rest of the word. Two painstaking minutes later, Angus pressed send, and the message flew off to the conference where Mum and Dad were teaching principles of Christian living. She knew that at this moment it was more important for Angus to be able to vent his anger in a safe place than to give him a lecture about language. That could come later, when the pain had passed, in the form of a conversation, which would be much more effective.

* * *

Some memories come to us for free, and these are memories that none of those grandmothers will lose. But most of our memories have to be initiated by us. In our family, we began a tradition when I took our eldest grandson, who was six at the time, to see *The Lion, the Witch and the Wardrobe* musical in London. Since then, I've continued to take each younger grandchild to a show for their sixth birthday. Now that the eldest grandchild is 13, we've started all over again. This time grandpa took him to *Les Misérables*, a show he already knew all the songs for. These birthday celebrations are definitely as big a deal for us as they are for the children, making us ridiculously over-the-top excited. (In fact, I wonder whether they secretly think, 'Oh please, Granny and Grandpa, you're so embarrassing.' Hmm.) They are treats in store as the years pass and each child becomes a teenager.

One of the obvious ways of fostering and strengthening relationships with our grandchildren is to create and build family traditions with them that open up time just to be together, times when space is made for conversation, regardless of whether those conversations happen. Of course, there are simpler ways of being together than going to a show – not to mention ways that leave the bank balance a lot less challenged. And there are ways with greatly reduced stress levels; the number of things that could spoil such expeditions is almost limitless – traffic, tummy-ache, home sickness, falling asleep (the grandchild, not me), falling over (me, not the grandchild). I whisper a deeply grateful prayer after each mission accomplished.

One of the best ways of getting to know a grandchild is having him or her to stay with you on their own. Many families, of course, get together at Christmas, and at other times of celebration, but often there are a lot of people milling around at such times and the chances of one of those connection bricks being added to the house of relationship are remote.

We often see our grandchildren for part of the school half-term breaks, and we do our best to hire a cottage for a week each summer, during which everyone is welcome. We also offer to look after the children so that their parents can celebrate wedding anniversaries, and enjoy the rare opportunity to have some time alone together – even if we can't imagine clearing the space, let alone having the energy to follow through on our offer when we make it!

As long as we have the strength, we'll receive as many grandchildren as our children are glad to lend us. And yes, it is tiring. We are a sight to behold after their departure, often sprawled on a sofa amid a sea of dolls, toy cars, Lego, the contents of the dressing-up box, assorted bits of plastic and stray topless felt-tips. We're lucky enough to have a children's spare room, which often looks as if there's been a heavy playing session for weeks after their departure. There's a notice on the door that reads, 'Nock [sic] if you want to come in.' It's been there for about four years and reminds me that I may not want to come in.

But I promise you the mess is worth every single item you have to pick up and every game you have to put back together. Most children behave better with their parents out of the way, even if they're rowdy and leave trails of mess everywhere. If you're someone who likes order and things in their rightful place, be warned: they won't be in their right place and there will be very little order while the troops are with you. We once spent months following a Christmas visit looking for the TV remote control and were very perplexed as to its whereabouts having turned the room in question upside-down several times. Then one day I was looking for something in the basement and came across my marmalade pan full of a random assortment of items, including tiny bits of Lego, a scarf from the dressing-up box and – you guessed it – the TV remote.

My mother famously relocated tea time with the grandchildren to the garage regardless of the weather (normally wild west-Wales coastal gales), and she obviously thought this was a great idea because it became one of our family's (less successful, not to mention chilly) traditions. We bore with it because we knew her need for order originated in some of her own childhood deprivations, but it was fairly frustrating, and did nothing to lessen the complicated morass of love and irritation that I felt towards her.

By now you will be thinking, 'This all takes a huge amount of effort, forethought, planning and, in the case of outings, money.' Yes, it does. And the truth is that although having a grandchild to stay is less expensive, it's hard not to spoil them, which often entails money. I remember taking my oldest grandson out for coffee (also known as fresh orange juice and Welsh rarebit) and when my change was returned found myself saying, 'Here you are, have a fiver.' What came over me?!

Anne, now in her 80s and with grown-up grandchildren, established the tradition of having her eight granddaughters to stay on their own from the age of four. Anne made a photographic record of each visit, sending the album to the granddaughter in question with the title *Now We Are Four*. She continued this tradition with *Now We Are Seven*; … *Eleven*; … *Fifteen*; and tells me they are forever asking for another – not surprisingly!

Mary writes about having grandchildren to stay:

Our second son has four children... The eldest, a girl, has stayed with us, without her parents, from an early age. Her brother likewise. Our relationship with our granddaughter, who is almost 15, has been a joy. She has stayed with us with a close cousin (not our granddaughter) and a girlfriend on several occasions. We have created traditions – going to the Cotswold Wildlife Park, for instance – which have been part of the familiarity of coming to stay.

Helen says of the traditions she and her husband are building with their grandchildren:

We play a game with our grandchildren that they love, where we tell them two true facts and one false fact about ourselves or their parents and they have to guess the false fact! This opens many conversations about rights and wrongs, ethics, good behaviour and much laughter!

I write to them from time to time telling them the things I love about them, and the things they are good at. I celebrate them and their uniqueness. As adults, when we meet to celebrate our birthdays, each of us in turn says something we love about the person whose birthday we are celebrating, and this is always moving as well as very funny! As the children get older I hope we will do the same for them.

On the occasions when I put the children to bed, we chat about how things are and what's going on and I pray with them. Some of them, especially the girls, have loads to say!

As time passes and grandparents and grandchildren grow older, the roles and responsibilities will slowly reverse. Until she moved in with one of her daughters at the age of 91, our children still visited my mother-in-law, now bringing the food themselves and sometimes cooking, rather than their grandmother doing all the work of hosting. The reason they made time to see her is that she had been very present in their childhood, often coming to stay and care for them while we were away working. Her generous gifts to us of these times with the children have reaped the fruit of our children's great affection for her as adults.

Back to the question of the investment we make in our grandchildren's lives – as we've seen, the research shows that love for grandparents isn't necessarily built into the grandparent–grandchild relationship, and that the onus for initiative in how we occupy the role lies with us. Unless we live very near our grandchildren and see them frequently, a close relationship isn't going to develop spontaneously.

In all this our attitude will be the vital factor. If we're remote and wait for our children to take the lead, it probably won't happen – not because our children don't want it to, but because simultaneously holding down a job and raising a family absorbs all their energy. On the other hand, we must take care not to be intrusive or to appear controlling. A reality check here wouldn't be a bad thing. We would do well to ask ourselves, 'Never mind not appearing controlling; what's in my heart really? Deep down, do I really think that if only they would take my advice, everything would be so much better and easier for them, because I've been there, done that and now know how to do it properly?'

The fact is we do *not* know best. Doing well in the grandparent role requires diplomacy, lots of patience and love that never runs out. We will say more about love later, but where keeping connected and developing close relationships with grandchildren are concerned, *be the giver who keeps on giving*. We need perseverance to keep pouring in the love and encouragement.

Visits and outings as described above are one way of doing this, but what about those of us who are separated from our grandchildren by thousands of miles? What about those whose home is too small to host small people? Without the reward of seeing the child and hugging them, without the reward of seeing a little face light up when you ask, 'Do you think I might have brought you a little present?', it's harder to keep the giving tap turned on, but it's essential if we want to know the people these children grow into.

You would think that no one needs to be reminded to mark a birthday or Christmas, but the advent of the internet and social media has radically changed our habits of communication, and fewer and fewer people send actual cards. Parents don't usually forget their own children, but children often forget their parents' birthdays once they are no longer being reminded by one parent to make a card for the other. Our grandchildren are unlikely to send us birthday cards, not least because in their eyes we're very old; while being 6 or 12 or 18 is hugely exciting, all ages above 30 blur into one 'old' number. Keeping the messages, letters and cards coming is our call; it's giving without counting the cost, giving without seeking a reward.

If we are faithful in sowing, I believe that one day the flowers will bloom. I must cite my mother-in-law again here. For many years, thanks to one of her daughters, who project manages this, she has had a photo calendar with photos of every member of her large family (15 grandchildren and 15 great-grandchildren and counting…) on the relevant month's page. She sends every one of them a card, including her children-in-law, though she has quite reasonably drawn the line at her grandchildren's spouses and partners. As a 90th birthday present, my three daughters gave her a bunch of flowers every month for a whole year. You will reap what you sow (though that is not *why* you sow).

As well as sending birthday and Christmas cards, we can also mark other rites of passage, such as starting nursery or school; becoming a teenager; leaving school; going to university or college or starting an apprenticeship or other training; or getting a first job. Before we know it, the cycle of human life is starting all over again and our first grandchild is getting married – or not as the case may be. (Lifestyle choices that are different from what we would wish for them, and the resulting challenge to remain unconditionally loving without abandoning our convictions, are the subject of another chapter.)

Beyond communicating by the traditional means of post or a phone call, there are now a plethora of means to keep in touch with our grandchildren. We can text, email, WhatsApp, Instagram, FaceTime, Skype and use various other methods of this proliferating technology. None of these are a patch on the real thing – you can't give them a hug through the screen; the connection may be poor; children may make conversation impossible in transcontinental calls; or it may just be hard to hear, which can lead to misunderstanding. It can be a minefield, but every ounce of effort is worth it.

Speaking of effort, here's what Isabel does to build memories with her eight grandchildren:

> My favourite thing is camping in the attic. Navy blue sheet from the roof as tent, sleeping bags on the floor, including for me, midnight feast and joke session (relax, you get the jokes from a joke book!) are the essentials, but lying in the dark and talking, sometimes for a long time ('Granny, tell me about…') is the best bit, as one by one they fall asleep.

No pressure there, then! I'm girding up my loins to emulate this fine example at the first opportunity; clearly the bar is set high.

> I taught the boys chess and the girls knitting – whoops, how un-PC is that?! We play competitive games when they come, and I usually cook with them. Shipwreck meals are a favourite. This involves unhealthy food and turning the furniture upside down. Sometimes we do gardening and we make bonfires nearly every time they're with us – good for chatting.

Not only are these things imaginative, but they're also inexpensive; the value of our memories and traditions doesn't depend on their cost.

And then there's reading to grandchildren, which was how I got to know Harry Potter, as well as revisiting the old classics of our youth. And cups of tea with sugar – shame on us! – sitting cosily in the grandparental bed with Beatrix Potter in the morning. And there are very simple, if naughty, traditions, like Grandpa's chocolate drawer.

It goes without saying that, although grandparents must be the sowers if they want to reap a good relationship with their grandchildren, parents exert a lot of influence and can facilitate the connections between grandparents and children. Again research comes up here with obvious conclusions, namely that where there's a close relationship between grandparents and their children, there's more likely to be a close relationship between grandparents and their grandchildren.

Adoption and fostering add another dimension to all this. Perhaps you are reading this as a grandparent to adopted or fostered children and are thinking about the unknowns that make grandparenting less predictable. After all, children who join a family any number of years after birth, or for only a short time, come with their own unfamiliar and often troubled history, so becoming family together is likely to be more of a challenge. But it really can happen, especially with God's help. 'God sets the lonely in families,' says the psalmist.[2] And adoption is at the very heart of the gospel: 'In love [God] predestined us for adoption to sonship through Jesus Christ.'[3] Mary writes:

> Our daughter and her husband adopted two boys, aged seven and five, several years ago. It's been a hugely challenging and rewarding journey. Before they arrived in our family, we created a 'who we are' book, to which all the grandchildren contributed, and went later, as a family unit, to the formal granting of their adoption. Over the years that they have been part of our family their trust has grown and both boys come to stay with us, and with their other grandparents, on their own. We have created familiar, but different, traditions with both of them. The older one is a thinker and processor,

so our conversations have ranged from God to bird-watching via some of the trauma that he has experienced. Our daughter has commented that they value the individual attention we give them, which was lacking in their past… I think the most important lesson we have learned is that our affection for these boys is not dependent on the fact that they are biologically related to us. In many ways our affection has a strength and quality that is different to the biological ones. Something to do with the grace of God.

Writing about another grandchild who came to live with her and her husband after the parents' marriage failed, she reflects that as well as the practical gestures of love, from birthday cakes to outings, what has really made the relationship between grandparents and grandchild secure has been their presence:

We have attempted to minister into the complexity of painful childhood struggles, which is an ongoing process. I think our 'ministry' as such has mainly been a presence that has led on occasion to important conversations.

All the very best memories and traditions must be soaked in two things to endure: the grace of God and our presence – that is, our being present in every contact, short or long, near or far, happy or sad. God's grace is guaranteed, but we can miss being present. To be present, we have to be listening, so let's think about that now.

3

The art of listening

Many people are looking for an ear that will listen. They do not find it among Christians, because these Christians are talking where they should be listening. But he who can no longer listen to his brother will soon be no longer listening to God either; he will be doing nothing but prattle in the presence of God too.

Dietrich Bonhoeffer[1]

Let the wise listen and add to their learning.

PROVERBS 1:5

I wonder whether we're in the habit of really hearing what our grandchildren are saying, bearing in mind that the words they speak may not reflect what they want to say, and that they may be feeling something deeply but struggling to put that feeling into words. Sometimes emotions are unexpectedly touched as people listen to each other, by things greater than our words. We need to be attentive.

A close friend lamented his failure to listen more carefully to his children, especially as they became adolescents and adopted grunt language. He acknowledged that fatigue and preoccupation with work were factors, as well as the irritation that rises with alarming ease in the parents of adolescents. Our world is a constant cacophony. It seems that few of us can tolerate silence, partly because it has become increasingly inaccessible, and partly because we are afraid of coming face-to-face with what lies within, so we keep ourselves distracted. If our reflex as adults is to lock down our inner world, how much more should we be attentive to our grandchildren's inner worlds, which may hold pain that could be coaxed to the surface with attentive listening?

Although many grandparents today are still working, we have often crested the hill of conquest; of believing we can make a significant impact in some area of life or work. We no longer believe we can save the world. We're more aware of our vulnerability, more aware of the fragility of human life. Unlike our children, we no longer have the unrelenting daily tasks that bringing up children entails, so perhaps we're more available to perceive what isn't said as well as what is. We have marginally fewer voices competing for our attention.

The Norwegian explorer Erling Kagge writes of the power of silence in his book *Silence: In the age of noise*. He describes meeting the entrepreneur Elon Musk, inventor of Tesla cars and at the forefront of revolutionising the energy and aerospace industries. After an initially disparaging reaction to the notion that silence is a blessing, Musk realised on reflection that he is someone who dwells in his own inner silence, often shutting out the world to open up his thoughts. The first place of consultation for Musk, where his visions and ideas are concerned, is the quiet space inside himself, not the experts who will declare what is possible and advise him to build on that.[2]

What does Elon Musk have to do with listening to our grandchildren? Musk experienced some hardships in his childhood, to which his response was to take refuge in his mind, where he was free to think for hours on end. He became familiar with his own inner space. All children experience some hardship. From teasing and bullying in the playground to competing for acceptance and comparing themselves with their peers in a hundred ways, children become familiar with their inner world. Even children who bully other children or are otherwise aggressive reveal that they know hardship, since such things are a response to fear, anger or pain. So we can be sure that every grandchild will have an inner world with which they are more or less familiar. They're unlikely to become world-famous entrepreneurs, but there are things to be heard if we listen carefully.

There are different kinds of hearing. There is active hearing and passive hearing. Active hearing only happens if we listen, and ask thoughtful, careful questions. How I wish I had not only understood but practised more active listening while my own children were growing up. They are so much better at listening to their children than I was at listening to them; I identify with my regretful friend.

Think about your grandchildren for a moment. How old are they? What are their family situations? How many siblings do they have? Where do they come in the family? Are they living with one parent or two? How demanding, in time and headspace, are the parents' jobs? Do you think they are able to find the time and space and attention needed to be able to put into words what they are thinking about and more importantly how they feel about anything?

Perhaps you are thinking, 'That's all very well, but how can I listen to my grandchildren when they live on another continent?' Or, 'How can I listen to my grandchildren when I have to look after them for part of every day, and I struggle with my diminishing energy? I just don't have the resources at the end of the day to coax the deep things out of their inner worlds.' Of course, there are as many variables where this question is concerned as there are grandchildren, but I believe we can tailor our listening to our own personal situation.

Perhaps just raising the topic can give you some food for thought. Maybe if you live far away and don't see your grandchildren very often, you can try to listen on Skype or, as literacy comes, by exchanging emails. Where little ones are concerned, make space for treat-time when you see them, and in between those times keep the loving communication flowing (via their parents or the post).

If, on the other hand, you see them all the time or look after them for part of the week, to succeed in active listening will be a challenge as we struggle with tiredness and battle with the inevitable conflicts that accompany child management. Even more difficult is being able to listen if we are the child's carer, as some grandparents are.

My prayer is that this will prompt you to reflect – do I listen to them at all at the moment? How could I make even the smallest space to see whether I can focus fully on one at a time?

And there is everything in between these two extremes. Your family and your situation are unique, and my hope is simply that you might be inspired to want to listen beyond the repetitive or whining demands of the toddler, the sullen silence of the teenager or the silence of the painfully shy child, and remember that what they say may not reflect what they mean or what they are feeling. Remember, too, that silence can speak louder than words, so listen to what isn't said as well as what is, and take note of body language.

Psychologists have pointed out that people can understand language about two or three times faster than they can speak. This implies that a listener has a lot of extra mental 'bandwidth' for thinking about other things while listening, but a good listener can use that spare capacity to stay focused on what the speaker is saying. Often we use it instead to think about our 'next move' in the conversation – our rebuttal or reply when the speaker stops – instead of focusing on understanding the speaker. Let's not do this with our grandchildren.

More depends on listening than on speaking. A skilful listener will know how to overcome the deficiencies of a vague or disorganised speaker – and children are often vague and distracted in their conversations. So the listener – that's you and me in this context – arguably bears more responsibility than the speaker for the quality of communication.

We live in a world in which people are much keener to speak than to listen – a world of soundbites and hurry. The BBC News app on my phone greets me in the morning with the question, 'In a hurry? Here's what you need to know this morning.' How much easier it is to interrupt or close down a child who wants to speak but is hesitant, than an adult.

So far we've looked at listening to our grandchildren themselves. What about listening to what God has to say about them or even to them? Helen says:

> When each of my nine grandchildren was a year old, I wrote what I thought were prophetic words that God had given me for them and gave them to their parents who have kept them.

As a grandparent who is a follower of Jesus, I make it my business to listen to God each day by reading his word, which I have elsewhere called his love letter to us. The book *A Year with Aslan* is a compilation of 365 short readings from 'The Chronicles of Narnia', each followed with some questions for reflection. In the preface, Michael Maudlin explains the motivation behind the book's publication:

> I grew up in a tradition that encouraged a daily practice of reading and reflection as a spiritual workout, and we often heard admonishments for why we had to will it earnestly and overcome our natural resistance to this vital practice. (In other words, it was presented as the spiritual equivalent of 'eat your vegetables'.) Yet this led me to the unexpected query, But what if I enjoyed it?[3]

For Maudlin, something that should be enjoyable and nourishing became – or perhaps always was from the beginning – dry and dreary, a task to be got through. Such things rarely develop our spiritual life, and can on the contrary drive us away from the very source of our spiritual flourishing. Many are those who have shaken off tedious religious routines, at school or at church, with joy and relief. *A Year with Aslan* was Maudlin's creative response to his boredom. Thinking about the effort and motivation required for good listening, this is a good opportunity to assess ourselves in relation to listening to God. How are you doing? And how are you doing it?

Like Maudlin, and many others, 'The Chronicles of Narnia' have become part of, as Maudlin says, the 'geography of my soul'. I write this just two days after watching *Prince Caspian* again. It never fails to touch my emotions and, finding it always so beautiful in what it conveys, I could hardly bear it and quickly swallowed the rising tears. I approach the Bible in the same spirit, asking that my hard heart and my weary soul be softened and tenderised, so that I can hear the call of Christ again and his words of encouragement to press on. I want to be touched to the core by what I read.

The Bible is not 'The Chronicles of Narnia'. (Indeed, without the Bible we would have no 'Chronicles of Narnia'.) The Bible is incomparably vaster, wiser, older; it is the offspring of Creator God, not of the mind of one of his creatures. The God-given imagination of C.S. Lewis, author of the Narnia stories, merely reflects some of the 'depth of the riches of the wisdom and knowledge of God'.[4] If a man can touch us through his writing, how much more can God awaken the depths of our souls with his words?

We can be touched to the core in all sorts of ways. We can become suddenly overwhelmed with the certainty that God loves us and that whatever happens nothing can ever change that, and we are forever held close. The strength of this may wax and wane, but we will not forget the moment. Or we can become suddenly and sharply aware of our shortcomings and be filled with a powerful longing to ask for forgiveness. The old word for this is repentance, which means to turn around and go the other way. Someone who has fallen into the habit of lying, for example, may experience an almost physical sensation, as the realisation hits them that to lie is profoundly wrong. Someone facing death may find a new power in the well-worn paths of Psalm 23: 'Even though I walk through the darkest valley, I will fear no evil.'[5]

All through history, men and women have had deep experiences, beyond words, of the love of God, and we can ask for such experiences, or epiphanies, too. As we become more practised at listening to God and try to make it a habit, like brushing our teeth, we can ask to hear messages for our grandchildren. What sort of thing might God say? A simple example can be found in Paul's letters to

Timothy: 'Don't let anyone look down on you because you are young, but set an example…'[6] Another example might be Jesus' words to the disciples that he will always be with them. Often in the Bible we find the words 'don't be afraid', which are apt for children, who often feel a bit fearful. Or, like my friend, we might hear something prophetic for a grandchild. Prophecy is a minefield and can easily be wrongly used. What does the Bible say? In his first letter to the Corinthians, whom Paul was having to rebuke on several fronts, he states firmly that prophecy must bring strength, encouragement and comfort.[7] And in the Old Testament, Jeremiah, himself a prophet, delivers harsh words from God to lying and false prophets who are speaking visions 'from their own minds'.[8]

Sometimes we may hear something that we sense is a message for a grandchild, but which we need to hold on to until we hear that it's time to pass it on. And this may be for years. We may have a sense of something that pertains to their future, but it's crucial that we don't use this to influence or manipulate their choices. Our goal is always to offer open-handed support and love, never to be controlling.

We can listen to our grandchildren, and we can listen to God for them. We can also listen to creation with them. 'The heavens declare the glory of God; the skies proclaim the work of his hands,' says David.[9]

> The starry sky is the truest friend in life, when you've first become acquainted; it is ever there, it gives ever peace, ever reminds you that your restlessness, your doubt, your pains are passing trivialities. The universe is and will remain unshaken.[10]

These are the words of a polar explorer, who does not himself recognise the source of what he describes, yet they evidence the fact that the skies speak of the vastness and the eternity of God, and that God is with us offering peace, perspective and even security amid the shaking of the nations.

Imaginative and creative dad Macneill Ferguson decided to have 100 adventures with his two small boys, Ollie and Harry. Aged five and eight at the time, they set their Playmobil pirate ship sailing from north-east Scotland in May 2017, and the little boat, filled with polystyrene and foam to prevent it sinking, made an epic journey round the globe. The boat was fitted with a state-of-the-art transmitter so that the brothers could follow its progress. Named *Adventure*, it sailed hundreds of kilometres from Scotland to Denmark, where it was set on its path again as instructed by the message aboard the vessel.

In late 2017, *Adventure* was once again relaunched off the coast of Mauritania and travelled almost 3,000 miles before its owners lost contact with it in May 2018, as the GPS battery died and the little vessel was overcome by churning currents and 65-foot high waves in the Caribbean.[11]

What an adventure for two small boys! But even more than the adventure itself, maybe these children and their parents will have found something bigger than the adventure; maybe they listened to creation and heard something beyond it – the sound of the creator walking in his garden.

I don't expect any grandparent, myself included, to launch uninvited into explanations regarding the ways in which God speaks through his creation. Though, of course, we can exclaim with our grandchildren at the beauty of a flower, beach, mountain or animal. We can comment on our artistic creator, on the beauty and truth of God's handiwork, and we can pray that it will speak to our grandchildren and seep into them. The kinds of conversations we have with our grandchildren will be shaped by their age and by circumstances, but every one of them invites the power of listening. I think our conversations as grandparents should be like snowflakes or stars – each one unique yet identifiable as good – and made beautiful by the quality of our listening.

4

This sunrise of wonder

Epiphanies, if we did but know it, lie like unopened gifts at every turn of the road and every stage of our journey.
Michael Mayne[1]

We saw his star when it rose and have come to worship him.
MATTHEW 2:2

Through the ages, wonderful men and women have succeeded in expressing deep and unsearchable things in such a way as to illumine the paths of others. Augustine of Hippo, Thomas Aquinas, Ignatius of Loyola, Benedict, Thomas à Kempis, Julian of Norwich, Teresa of Avila, John of the Cross – these are names that I love to pronounce, because they evoke both the mists of time and the depths of truth; and many of them have a romantic ring to them. But more than their names, it is their writings that unfold mysteries, and each shines another shaft of light on the whole.

Jumping forward a few centuries, we come to the great 20th-century contributors in this genealogy of Christian writers, such as George MacDonald, G.K. Chesterton, Dietrich Bonhoeffer, J.R.R Tolkien and C.S. Lewis. Poets and painters have also expressed their faith in Christ across the centuries, their creativity replicating that of their creator. Think of the metaphysical poets, such as John Donne and George Herbert, exalting God in their lines and rhymes, or the writings of the war poets – Siegfried Sassoon, Wilfred Owen, Robert Graves, Rupert

Brooke and others. Or consider works such as Rembrandt's huge *The Return of the Prodigal Son* in the Hermitage Museum, Saint Petersburg, or Michelangelo's ceiling of the Sistine Chapel in the Vatican. The list is endless, but the men and women of history who spoke their faith in one way or another offer a wealth of truth and beauty to which we might introduce our grandchildren.

Of particular pleasure to me are the works of C.S. Lewis, and they are still a top choice for connecting with my grandchildren. Even in this age of post-truth, when things of the 1950s are deemed curiously old-fashioned and fading fast into the mists of time, Lewis' evocation of Christianity through the Narnia stories still has the power to touch hearts, and spring our deepest longings for eternity and heaven.

This life is full of wonder: people and places; art and architecture; heroes and history; courage and compassion. But the greatest wonder of all is to know God, the creator of it all – to glimpse holiness and catch sight of the sacred. I dream of one day being able to help my grandchildren grasp the amazing truth that it's possible for men and women to encounter God and become his friend. I'm probably dreaming of lots of different days, rather than just 'one day' – perhaps as we sit round a bonfire on Guy Fawkes Night, cooking marshmallows; or as we walk along a windy beach; or as we sit in a cafe, sipping steaming hot chocolate topped with cream; or when, as young adults, they come to 'The Grandparents Bash', a tradition lovingly maintained by some dear older friends, who invite their now adult grandchildren to 'pizza and plonk' every year. Whenever, wherever and with whichever grandchildren it might happen, I pray that it does. I dream of agreeing with them that God really does exist.

Interestingly, unless they have been clearly persuaded otherwise, all children have an instinctive trust in the reality of God. In his book *This Sunrise of Wonder*, Michael Mayne writes of this. Describing humanity's deep, if often overlaid, affinity with the transcendent and the numinous, he quotes Gerard Manley Hopkins, writing of our world as 'charged with the grandeur of God. It will flame out, like shining from shook foil,'[2] and also Isaiah, who says, 'The whole earth is full of his glory.'[3] Mayne writes, 'There is a sense in which children, who live on what is given anew at every moment, have this kind of vision too.'[4]

That God exists is one thing, but if he does what's he like? I want to tell my descendants – children, teens and adults – that by far the most important truth about God is that he is love. God loves every human being and yearns for communion with her or him.

> Dear friends [and grandchildren], let us love one another, for love comes from God. Everyone who loves has been born of God and knows God.[5]

I picture talking with my grandchildren about what God is like in other ways, too. God is at once so much bigger than us and so different from us, the one who made the whole world to infinity and beyond, but at the same time God is the one who loves each of us more than we can comprehend. Maybe we'll chat about who else apart from God loves us more than we can really grasp, and about who we love more than we can really put into words, and what this feels like. Naturally, these thoughts, and answers to the questions they raise, will depend on the age and stage of the grandchild in question. Who loves me more than I can imagine? Mummy and Daddy; my best friend; my boyfriend; my girlfriend; my partner. But considering how hard it is to describe the depths of love, I hope we might get to agree that when it comes to God, we're talking about a different league of love altogether.

The apostle Paul writes, 'The Son is the image of the invisible God.'[6] If this is true, and I believe it is, it means that God has opened a door through which we can look and begin to understand how amazing, how loving, how breathtaking he is. That door is Jesus. We can look through Jesus and see God, and we can invest in a relationship with God because of Jesus. Jesus expands on this image in John's gospel, saying, 'I am the gate for the sheep… I am the gate; whoever enters through me will be saved.'[7]

Now, back to what I aspire to pass on to my grandchildren…

In his gospel, John tells us that the Holy Spirit, the spirit of God and Jesus, is accessible to every human being. Since his ascension, Jesus has no longer been confined to one human body; there is now a new paradigm: 'Anyone who loves me… My Father will love them, and we will come to them and make our home with them.'[8]

Let's just pause for a minute – this is a mind-bending concept! The essence of a real person, Jesus, and of God who is completely 'other', can be known by men, women and children. The essence of a person is their spirit, and we call the essence of God and Jesus the Holy Spirit, because it is both the spirit of God the Father and the spirit of Jesus the Son. This is hard to understand, but when you encounter Jesus, you know it. And it's a wonder. All sorts of things are hard to understand, even falling in love. To others, the person you are obsessed with – in whose company you want to be all the time, about whom you cannot stop talking, who makes your stomach turn over, your cheeks blush and your heart beat faster – may seem ordinary and uninteresting, but you are in the grip of an overwhelmingly powerful attraction. This is how it can be with God.

It happened to me over 40 years ago, but I can still remember the wonder and the headiness as if it was the other day. I'd gone to Cambridge for a postgraduate year to qualify as a teacher and had arrived there on the back of a difficult rejection by my boyfriend of some years, so I was floundering emotionally. There's nothing like rejection to inundate one with insecurity and self-doubt, but I was taken in by three Christians who were just like the sisters of *Little Women* in their friendliness and freshness. Their small community provided a sharp contrast with the lifestyle I'd left behind in Oxford. The adjective 'godly' seems appropriate for these young women, so utterly different were they from my other student friends.

They gave me five-star care, which made a huge impression on me. Perhaps a lot of it was due to the startling difference between selfishness and unselfishness. Parallel with my new college life, an inner journey was starting: I 'fell among Christians' as they introduced me to all their friends, and I found myself hearing about God and Jesus and what being a Christian was all about, and asking a thousand questions in response. I was a difficult customer, objecting to almost everything, and interrupting Bible studies and prayer meetings with hostility and without qualm. Life as a student is the time during which we are perhaps most open to ideas and discussions around otherwise taboo subjects. As the years pass, our convictions settle down and often harden, like drying glue.

When I wasn't vigorously debating and arguing with my Christian friends, I plunged myself into amateur theatre – a very different scene and a much less 'clean' one. My soul was on the threshing floor, until one night, four months into the course, when I was living in my own student accommodation, as I was drifting off to sleep, something suddenly caused me to leap from my bed and then kneel beside it. I knew instantly that this was the invisible yet tangible presence of God filling the room, and I surrendered to him with the unlikely words, 'Okay, God, you win.' Not really polite, considering the company, and certainly not eloquent. No theology either. But I knew absolutely that my life turned on a hinge in those moments, and so it has proved to be. I would be forever in the grip of an overwhelmingly powerful attraction. Every aspect of life from that evening encounter onwards changed direction, and while my years have included times of desperation and distress, the rivers have not swept over me, and the flames have not set me ablaze.[9] If this happened to me, it can happen to anyone, and I hope and pray that it will be granted to me to tell each of my grandchildren this story one day.

In a family familiar with the practices of Christianity, children might ask some enchanting questions about God, but talk of theology comes rarely in the bustling days in which we live. If it does, it can be whisked away as suddenly as it arrives by the arrival of someone else, or a squabble breaking out, or someone getting hurt, or any sort of domestic activity around food or arrangements.

I pray for at least one treasured conversation with each grandchild in God's time. As the psalmist says, 'My times are in your hands.'[10] Questions about elusive and ephemeral things, such as my account above, are a challenge to answer. 'What do you mean you asked Jesus to come and live in you by his Spirit? How does that work?' My own answer would be something along the lines of, 'I don't really know how God's Spirit got into me. I just know that when I gave up my independence in that short prayer, something happened that changed the direction of my life, and that I felt different.' I might also talk about clever Nicodemus, who asked a similar question – 'How can someone be born when they are old?'[11] – and have a look with the grandchild in question at Jesus' answer. And I might talk about 'surrender', which is a good word, if an old one, because it conveys the sense of giving in or yielding, something we are so resistant to. And I was super-resistant!

What does this friendship bring with it? A trustworthy companion for life's journey; a safe place; the marvel and freedom of forgiveness. It reignites my capacity to love if it's been shut down, and strengthens it if it's been active. It reminds me that I was designed to live forever, and that eternal life, as opposed to existence, begins when I decide to follow him. As Jesus prayed, 'Now this is eternal life: that they know you, the only true God, and Jesus Christ, whom you have sent.'[12]

Later on, after the roller-coaster events of the crucifixion and the resurrection, the apostle John was able to write in his letter, 'This is love: not that we loved God, but that he loved us, and sent his Son… We love because he first loved us.'[13] John was known as the beloved disciple, he who had enjoyed one of the closest relationships with Jesus. Like the rest of the disciples, John initially hadn't been able to believe the women who came breathlessly racing back from the tomb to tell the dejected men that it was empty, and that they had seen Jesus.[14] Their words had seemed like nonsense, and how easy it is to be cynical and disbelieving when life is dark and all your hopes and dreams have been shattered. But John saw for himself, soon after this climactic moment, and everything changed; when he writes about God being love, you can hear the conviction in his voice.

Like John, I was cynical and unconvinced for a long time, and things were dark for me. I felt unloved and insecure. But then I, too, saw for myself; I encountered the risen Christ and it changed everything. I knew for certain that it was God who made me with love, just as he made every other human being ever created, and that I was made for a purpose and was filled with potential. I knew that God was for us and that he can be known, because I had met him.

By definition, experience is subjective and proves nothing. Yet life is full of things whose existence is indisputable but for which there is no empirical proof – love, trust, faith, hope. For all these, there is proof only in acts of love, trust, faith or hope. These come mostly in small, unnoticed moments of people's lives, and occasionally in bigger events that come to the world's notice.

If I am a friend of Jesus, what do I learn from him that I'd like to pass on? John's gospel concludes, 'Jesus did many other things as well. If every one of them were written down, I suppose that even the whole world would not have room for the books that would be written.'[15] Everything about Jesus is appealing: his compassion, courage, vulnerability, strength, integrity, directness, priorities, wisdom, brilliance and sacrifice. Let's look at just a few of these characteristics.

The compassion of Jesus

As Jesus heals, we can sometimes see that he feels. In the story of the woman with an issue of blood,[16] for example, Jesus' capacity to care so fully for one sick woman, exhausted by a twelve-year pursuit of healing, shines through the text. Kindness and compassion are close relatives. We can be undone by kindness, and a small act of kindness can have a big impact. I once contacted a pastor, hoping desperately to reconnect with someone I had lost all sight of through sad circumstances. I didn't expect this busy pastor to call me back, let alone hear my heart as he did, and the compassion in his voice moved me to tears. Then there is kindness that bestrides the world, such as that of Mother Teresa, who gave her life to loving the poor and the unlovely, the sick and the destitute, or of Paul Brand, who devoted his life to pioneering treatment for leprosy, having realised the paradoxical value of pain.

The courage of Jesus

Courage is not the same as bravery. Jesus was certainly brave, but let's pray that his courage in facing the religious leaders of his day and in challenging their hypocrisy sets his word in our hearts like a fire,[17] expanding our own courage.

The film *Hacksaw Ridge* (2016) tells the real-life story of Desmond Doss, a pacifist who, while he wouldn't use a weapon because of his religious convictions, nonetheless persisted in being called up for military service. Present at the battle of Okinawa as a combat medic, Doss remained among the wounded for longer than anyone else, and in scenes of incomprehensible violence and bloodshed, rescued 75 men from death. He became the first conscientious objector to be awarded the US Medal of Honor, for service above and beyond the call of duty. I am renowned in my family for my aversion to seeing violence in movies, so the news that I was looking forward to seeing *Hacksaw Ridge* was greeted with cries of 'You won't like it, Mum; it's really violent.' But I wanted to see it because I knew it was a story of honour and courage. There *is* a lot of violence, as men's bodies are torn to shreds, scenes that make one recoil. But that is the reality of war, and in this story the violence is not gratuitous. At the end of it, I found myself strangely moved and stirred, lifted despite the gruesome scenes by a young man risking his life to save others. Such acts of self-sacrifice touch something deep in the soul, because they connect into the sacrifice that Jesus made for all humanity. And they draw us into wonder at the heights of human nobility in the face of the depths of human depravity.

History is laced with outstanding examples of men and women demonstrating that sometimes a life has to be lost in order for another to be saved. William Tyndale, James Hannington, Edith Cavell, Anne Frank, Maximilian Kolbe, Martin Luther King, Jr – all gave their lives for righteousness and to save others. Less well known is the self-sacrifice of many engineers on the *RMS Titanic*. Together they point to the one life that was given for all lives.

The integrity of Jesus

Integrity is hard to define and doesn't yield an adjective. It has to do with being whole and undivided. It includes uprightness, unity, coherence, cohesion, morality, truthfulness and lack of corruption. A biblical rendering is 'holding together': 'In him all things hold together.'[18] The integrity of a plane keeps it airborne. Billy Graham said:

> Integrity is the glue that holds our way of life together. We must constantly strive to keep our integrity intact. When wealth is lost, nothing is lost; when health is lost, something is lost; when character is lost, all is lost.[19]

The Bible puts it like this: 'Many claim to have unfailing love, but a faithful person who can find? The righteous lead blameless lives; blessed are their children after them.'[20] This expresses the challenge it is to preserve integrity and is as true for grandparents as for parents. It applies to small moments – did I really pay attention when being shown the picture proudly drawn? Did I listen to the stumbling story that took a while to tell when I was in a hurry to do something else? – as well as to larger things, such as how we behave towards our grandchildren, towards their parents or indeed towards one another.

People who inspire us about these things are carrying the presence of Christ. The apostle Paul was able to say, 'We are to God the pleasing aroma of Christ.'[21] This is the kind of person I would like to be. Wouldn't you?

* * *

If we want to be the kind of grandparent who inspires and attracts our grandchildren, what better thing to do than look at the character of Christ? He embodies everything noble and exemplifies the gifts of the Spirit listed in Paul's letter to the Galatians: 'love, joy, peace, forbearance, kindness, goodness, faithfulness, gentleness and self-control. Against such things there is no law.'[22]

Often people drift away from their roots because opportunities to explore them don't arise. In today's world, Christians are often diffident about matters of faith, and unless we find our way, or are invited, into a context that welcomes such questions as 'What do you actually *mean* by saying God turned himself into a man? How can a person's spirit get into another person? How do you know when his Spirit is in you?', we're not likely to answer them.

As a Christian, then, captivated by Jesus, these are the things I want to pass on to my grandchildren. But if we hope that our grandchildren will find the idea of friendship with Jesus attractive, we'd better do our best to imitate him, which means knowing from the start that we'll need to become expert at apologising. The most important thing we'll pass on is what we are, rather than what we say; that is, what we do, how we do it and what we don't do – who we are as we aspire to somehow transmit our faith – is so much more important than our words. Our demeanour is the determining factor. Am I fun to be with? Am I strict, grumpy, sharp or too tired to listen properly?

It's tempting to feel defeated at the thought of this. Embarking on this project has made me reflect on my own parenting, and it's often an uncomfortable experience, as some painful memories surface. To my shame, an oft-quoted event in the annals of our family history is 'the time Mum hit Jack over the head with a barbecue'. I confess that I have had the temerity to lecture on raising children, and that this story received a laugh when one of my daughters, who was giving the child's perspective as part of the talk, followed my assertion that I was always quick to say sorry with the example, 'When she hit Jack over the head with a barbecue, she was really, really sorry.' (The barbecue in question was a small disposable tinfoil one. This is not to suggest that it was therefore fine to hit him with it; rather, to reassure you that he survived the assault.)

It's who we are that counts, not what we say. Famously, it is said that where communication is concerned, words account for 7%, tone of voice for 38% and body language for 55%.

Nothing we do or say in their company is invisible to or goes unnoticed by children, who are very observant and will report back to their parents on the slightest deviation from expected behaviour. I once gently suggested to one of my granddaughters that she be a little more generous in expressing her thanks for something (to someone else). This was immediately reported and translated into, 'Granny told me I had to write a card and say thank you.' That was certainly her impression, and perhaps I was a bit out of line, caring more about what the person in question might think of my granddaughter than about letting a nine-year-old develop her own ways of expressing herself. It's challenging to strike the right balance between encouraging respect and generosity and watching a child learn to be true to themself.

While we are all painfully aware of our own shortcomings, and the dark places in our souls, we also know that humanity is capable of greatness and goodness; history shows us many examples. I am sure that, like me, you have sometimes met or learned about a person, past or present, who triggers a deep response in the depths of your being. You might feel inspired or tearful, or you might have, in Wordsworth's phrase, momentary 'intimations of immortality'. Something about them might make you say, 'I want to be like you when I grow up.' I still say that about one of my most admired friends, who is 20 years ahead of me on the road. We will have a natural desire to ask questions of this person, because we want to emulate them in some way, and we have a momentary flash of understanding about our poverty of spirit as we see them, watch them or learn about them. But let's not forget that you and I are also capable of great goodness and generosity. I know that God says of you, too, 'You are my beloved child; well done, good and faithful servant.'[23]

Hope is an elusive idea to grasp, but is often something given in extreme circumstances, when common sense would say that all is lost or when darkness seems to be closing in. Sometimes it is literal darkness – think of those who have been imprisoned, either as hostages or political prisoners, for long periods and have told the story when set free, such as Terry Waite, Richard Wurmbrand, Nelson Mandela and Immaculée Ilibagiza, the Rwandan–American author and motivational speaker, whose autobiography recounts how she survived during the Rwandan genocide.[24] So many people have no hope or have lost what hope they once had, but in spite of the overwhelming levels of injustice and suffering that we are made aware of, I want to tell my grandchildren that in this confusing world, where boundaries shift like fog every day, there is in fact a great hope.

And that hope is this: because God became a man in Jesus, so that we could understand him and relate to him, we can grow a lifelong friendship with him, a friendship that nothing can break. You can't offend Jesus so that he 'unfriends' you. You can wound him, but he will never reject you.

I may not get much chance to talk about all this, though I hope and pray that my grandchildren will feel confident enough of my love and approval to ask questions and initiate conversations as the years go by. I want to tell them that God made a beautiful world, and that although we have managed to deface and damage it in many ways, many people still find him in the natural beauty of his creation.

I want to tell them that God is kind, that God is good, and that all our feelings of and impulses towards love come from him, because he has embedded the capacity to love within the human heart. I want to tell them that God loves every human being regardless of race, religion, sexual identity or any other difference, and regardless of whether the individual recognises or believes in him. I want to tell them that every person in all of time, past, present and future, was, is and will be completely loved by God; that because of this, I and they can live a life of love and giving.

5

A grandparent's creed

I believe in Christianity as I believe that the sun has risen, not only because I see it but because by it I see everything else.
C.S. Lewis[1]

The Son of Man came to seek and to save the lost.
LUKE 19:10 (ESV)

It's been said that it took 500 years to implant Christianity in the west and, 1,500 years later, only 50 years to uproot it. The seeds for this were laid 300 years ago at the time of the Enlightenment, a time that drew people towards the primacy of human reason, thus paving the way for a rejection of objective, universal truth. So began the journey towards individualism and the 'iWorld' we all inhabit today.

Since the mid-1990s, we've seen an acceleration in the rate of change. A major factor in this has been the expansion of the internet, which, although it has brought improvements to the lives of many through faster and more efficient systems of communication, has also brought harmful things, such as the Dark Web, an exponential growth in the porn industry and the wide dissemination of extreme political views. The advent of the smartphone has made social media pre-eminent in relationships, and that too has resulted in both good and bad – for example, public bullying, giving rise to the term 'trolling', has sometimes led to a tragic loss of life. Less immediately shocking, but with as yet unknown consequences, the smartphone has also opened the way to identity theft through mediums like Facebook.

With opinions and convictions able to go viral, public opinion has become more powerful and social changes have happened faster. We've experienced a radical shifting of boundaries with regard to identity and sexuality, and a profound rejection of societal and generational norms. All of this has taken place within the past 30 years or so, and at the time of writing, the result of the 2016 Brexit referendum is taking its toll in a widely felt uncertainty about national values.

It's against this background that, like so many grandparents, I live my longings for my grandchildren. And yes, I think we worry about them. Juliet says:

> It's not that I don't know what to *do* with my grandkids! That's easy: pray and love and be there and help out (and sometimes spoil), etc. It's that I don't know how to *feel*.

> I have so much love invested in them, and find I am in a state of fear and anxiety as they grow up. I want some reassurance of God's grace and mercy and that prayer works. I want to switch my fear to hope!

> It is so, so complicated in this world of technology; I know I am a technophobe and don't have faith that it can do them any good.

For many families living in what some call post-Christendom and in an age of post-truth, it's no longer a given that generation will unquestioningly follow generation along the paths of faith. In this chapter, we will look at the theological content of what we want to pass on – what we believe and why we believe it. We long for our grandchildren to make friends with God, so what is it that we would love them to think about, talk about and probably wrestle with?

We often speak in generalities, making it hard to grasp the heart of what we actually believe, and behind this I sense a subconscious diffidence, which is perhaps the fruit of a subtle but society-wide sidelining of Christianity. What better place to go for the bare bones of our faith than the Apostles' Creed, an ancient summary of Christianity that contains the essential teaching of the twelve apostles, Jesus' earliest followers?

I believe in God, the Father Almighty,
Creator of heaven and earth.

In a friend's seaside cottage, where I wrote part of this book, there is a painting of a gypsy caravan with lighted windows under the shelter of a great tree. A crescent moon lights the night scene. Underneath is written:

I loved it… when I was tucked up in bed and my father was telling me stories. Most wonderful of all was the feeling that when I went to sleep, my father would still be there, very close to me.

Captured in both picture and words is the universal longing for love, warmth and protection, and for a father.

There are good fathers and bad fathers, kind fathers and cruel fathers, and our grandchildren will come to know that not all fathers are safe. It may be that you are reading this with the pain of knowing that your own son is not a good father, or with regrets about your own fathering. As we tell our grandchildren the story of the prodigal son, we can be telling it to ourselves: the story of a perfect father, a father who offers emotional safety and consistency, who will never change or leave, and best of all whose constant loving presence can be uninterruptedly known. Like the father in Jesus' story, this father is also always scanning the horizon and waiting with open arms for a lost child to return. At a moment's notice he will hitch up his robes and run to sweep the returning child up into his arms. God is the ultimate and universal Father, and in Jesus he offers us all the love, warmth and protection that we long for.

In tandem with the gradual marginalisation of Christianity, the opening years of the 21st century have seen people openly and unashamedly interested in spirituality, and it's almost as if God is all the rage – God 'whoever you conceive him to be', as the excellent AA programme puts it, whether Gaia, or Mother Earth, or any other description. All human beings have a homing instinct for the supernatural, being made of spirit as well as flesh and bones; of unseen things like conscience, soul and spirit, as well as the visible human form. 'Spirit can only speak through matter. When I was born, my physical body became the vehicle of the spiritual being I know myself to be.'[2] So this search for spiritual meaning should not surprise us.

Right at the beginning of the Bible we read in the creation story that 'God saw all that he had made, and it was very good'.[3] This Father is also creator. The natural world is a thing of staggering beauty, and many of us become attuned to the presence of God when, far from the madding crowd, in nature's wide-open spaces, we are willingly overcome by the beauty of creation. The seasonal cycles of nature fill us with wonder. Just a few feet outside my window, as I write this in June, sprigs are forming on the chestnut tree that is hundreds of years old. At the other end of the year, in November, the rich mantle of leaves will be gone – turned golden brown and fallen after the full-grown conkers – but the naked tree will still be striking and beautiful. I hope that my grandchildren will notice such small things, as well as seeing the horizon. I hope they will be filled with wonder at both the marvels and the intricacies of creation.

I believe in Jesus Christ, his only son our Lord,
Who was conceived by the Holy Spirit,
Born of the Virgin Mary.

If God is all the rage, Jesus is more problematic. While many will say they believe in God and are even open to the idea of the Holy Spirit, increasingly Jesus has become a stumbling block. People say, 'I just don't get the Jesus bit.' This is obviously truer of younger generations, Gen X, millennials and Gen Y, born and raised in the so-called post-truth culture.

Father Raniero Cantalamessa, Preacher to the Papal Household since 1980, serving under popes John Paul II, Benedict XVI and Francis, has often said, 'The battle today is around Jesus.'[4] Just as during Jesus' life on earth and the beginnings of the early church, it is the uniqueness of Jesus that causes offence.

The pages of the Bible are filled with exceptional people – think of Moses, Joshua, Elijah, Esther, Deborah, John the Baptist – yet not one of them was like Jesus. Jesus is unique; he alone is the universal Saviour, and he alone was the child of one physical and one spiritual parent. He is wholly God and wholly man. He is a paradox. Napoleon Bonaparte said, 'I know men and I tell you that Jesus Christ is no mere man. Between him and every other person in the world there is no possible term of comparison.'[5] Jesus is different from every other human being who has ever lived. As journalist Anthony Burgess wrote, Jesus 'remains, to say the least of it, unique. If God is like Jesus, God is worth believing in.'[6]

> This is how God showed his love among us: he sent his one and only Son into the world that we might live through him.[7]

How did he do this? God, who is other and defies description by any of our common measurements, minimised himself and entered the womb of a virgin as an embryo created from a human egg and the Spirit of God. Did the Holy Spirit create sperm in the same way that he said, 'Let there be light' and there was light? We cannot know *how* he did it exactly, but we can know *that* he did it; a historical human called Jesus was born.

> What is uniquely Christian is not simply the belief that God meets us in a personal encounter, but the belief that this… God was once revealed in the only language we can understand: in human language, and in a human life. It is the belief that Jesus, alone of all our race, looked full at the transcendent mystery and said his name was Father.[8]

This folding of the infinite into the finite space of a womb is immortalised in John Donne's sonnet 'Annunciation':

> Salvation to all that will is nigh;
> That All, which always is all everywhere,
> Which cannot sin, and yet all sins must bear,
> Which cannot die, yet cannot choose but die,
> Lo, faithful virgin, yields Himself to lie
> In prison, in thy womb; and though He there
> Can take no sin, nor thou give, yet He will wear,
> Taken from thence, flesh, which death's force may try.
> Ere by the spheres time was created, thou
> Wast in His mind, who is thy Son and Brother;
> Whom thou conceivst, conceived; yea thou art now
> Thy Maker's maker, and thy Father's mother;
> Thou hast light in dark, and shutst in little room,
> Immensity cloistered in thy dear womb.[9]

> **He suffered under Pontius Pilate,**
> **Was crucified, died and was buried;**
> **He descended to the dead.**
> **On the third day he rose again;**
> **He ascended into heaven**

Today's relativism and individualism dictate that there can be no overarching truth about the universe; we can invent our own rationale of existence, and in the name of tolerance no one has the right to gainsay us. The idea, therefore, that one man, Jesus, died for the whole human race, past, present and future, can understandably be an offence to the modern mind. But Jesus is not one among many; Christians believe he is the universal Saviour, because he freely gave up his life to open the way for humankind to relate meaningfully to God, and alone of all humanity defeated death.

John's gospel carries one of the most well-known verses in the Bible: 'God so loved the world that he gave his one and only Son, that whoever believes in him shall not perish but have eternal life.' Eugene Peterson puts it like this: 'This is how much God loved the world: He gave his Son, his one and only Son. And this is why: so that no one need be destroyed; by believing in him, anyone can have a whole and lasting life.'[10]

We may object and ask, why should anyone perish? I don't know about you, but I know that in me lurk all kinds of things I have needed, and will need, forgiveness for and saving from: angry thoughts and outbursts, self-pity, carping criticism. I am as capable of having a wrong or unkind reaction as I am of having a right and kind one. Aren't you? Really? I think if honesty prevailed, the list for most of us would be long. In my case, I'm just one ordinary person. Multiply that by history's record of human cruelty and the sheer immeasurable volume of evil begins to help the notion of salvation make sense.

In giving his life for humankind, Jesus, who unlike you and me never had a sinful thought, let alone ever committed a sinful act, fulfilled his own words, 'Greater love has no one than this: to lay down one's life for one's friends.'[11] This was not an appropriate punishment, but an unspeakably amazing free gift. 'Thanks be to God for his indescribable gift,' writes the apostle Paul to the Corinthians.[12]

I want my grandchildren to see the beauty and the majesty of this worldwide, history-long gift and to see that, far from being an unnecessary and excluding act of destruction, it was the turning point of the ages. Jesus pre-existed the whole creation, as Paul writes: 'The Son is the image of the invisible God, the firstborn over all creation. For in him all things were created... and for him. He is before all things, and in him all things hold together.'[13] The vastness and inclusivity of Jesus' self-sacrifice is literally indescribable and invaluable – this is what I pray that my grandchildren might somehow see and catch.

I want them to know that the extraordinary truths of Jesus' crucifixion and resurrection sing out the message that God loves every human being – no exceptions; no exclusions. And you don't have to believe in God to be loved by him. You cannot not be loved. Jesus opens the way to knowing God as Father and friend, he who:

> had equal status with God but didn't think so much of himself that he had to cling to the advantages of that status no matter what. Not at all. When the time came, he set aside the privileges of deity and took on the status of a slave, became *human*! Having become human, he stayed human. It was an incredibly humbling process. He didn't claim special privileges. Instead, he lived a selfless, obedient life and then died a selfless, obedient death – and the worst kind of death at that – a crucifixion.[14]

This is why Jesus could say, 'I am the way.'[15] The human heart can't be cured by reason or effort. The Bible is clear that humanity's default reflex is towards evil, aggression, wrong and conflict. Long ago, at the beginning, 'The Lord saw how great the wickedness of the human race had become on the earth, and that every inclination of the thoughts of the human heart was only evil all the time.'[16] This is echoed by Jeremiah: 'The heart is deceitful above all things and beyond cure. Who can understand it?'[17]

Ever since we decided that we wanted the knowledge of good and evil,[18] the human race has been incapable of resisting evil. A logical question to follow this is: why did God put the tree of the knowledge of good and evil in the garden of Eden in the first place? Why deliberately place temptation in our way? Well, was it temptation, or was it rather for our protection? When we put a stairgate at the top of our stairs, it's not to tempt our toddler to find out how it opens and operate it.

There is something about submission, something about freedom of choice and something about authority in the story of the garden of Eden. When the serpent says to the woman, 'When you eat from it your eyes will be opened, and you will be like God,'[19] he doesn't mean that they would be full of mercy, grace, justice, peace and 'whatever is true… noble… right… pure… lovely… admirable'.[20] Rather, he means that they would be like God because they would be his equal, in power and knowledge.

Money, sex and power are our greatest cravings, dressed up in all manner of guises. The desire for all these lies deep in the human heart and has been there since the beginning. Leaving the fruit whole would have altered the entire course of human history – it would have led to harmony and life without end and without death, as we know it. But the bite was taken and the blaming began.

The consequences of falling for the temptation to be equal with God then unfold: banishment from the garden, leading to the loss of eternal life on earth; struggles in production and reproduction; and most significantly, alienation between man and woman. We see all these more than evidenced today, over 20 centuries on from these old stories.

I don't think any of us would deny the power of temptation – the overwhelming urge to buy, to drink, to have sex, to use a substance. Equally, I don't think anyone would deny there is a difference between good and bad practice of those activities – buying things is necessary; having a drink with a friend is sociable; sex is a beautiful thing; curative medicines are beneficial.

A note here as we pass: I believe that God intended sex to be enjoyed in the context and confines of marriage, and I believe that this is what the Bible teaches in both Old and New Testaments.[21] But I know (and love) other Christians who wouldn't agree with me.[22] With regards to grandchildren, my longing here is simply to be able to communicate my own convictions for consideration. No one can make anyone else believe anything. Sex and sexuality are complex and controversial subjects, never more so than today, so let's tread softly and lovingly. Perhaps here more than anywhere else, who I am matters more than what I say.

How should we define the difference between good and bad usage? Back in Genesis, when the first fights happened, God said to Cain, '[Sin] desires to have you, but you must rule over it.'[23] The very next verse records the murder of Abel by Cain. He did not master sin, but sin 'had him'. The difference must lie in an inability to do what is right, something that Paul laments in his own life, acknowledging that the only way he can overcome sin is with the help of Jesus:

> What I don't understand about myself is that I decide one way, but then I act another, doing things I absolutely despise... and if the power of sin within me keeps sabotaging my best intentions, I obviously need help! I decide to do good, but I don't *really* do it; I decide not to do bad, but then I do it anyway... Something has gone wrong deep within me and gets the better of me every time.[24]

Perhaps we are at a point where we can define sin as doing wrong, doing things to excess and without boundaries or self-control, or doing things with aggression or because of addiction. There are some things for which there is no good practice, things that are always wholly bad and wrong and for which moderation is irrelevant – for example, taking life, adultery, theft, false testimony and envy; these are enshrined in the ten commandments, recorded in Exodus 20.

Jesus, of course, refines the meaning of wrongdoing, extending it beyond action to thoughts. It's not just expressing my envy that's wrong; it's also enjoying it in the safe privacy of my thoughts. It's because of our inability to overcome the pull of sin that Jesus laid down his life to give us freedom from it.

In trying to unpack the difference between right and wrong, and thinking through hypothetical conversations with grandchildren, I've used the word 'sin'. Like so many words it has become overlaid with other, derogatory and negative, meanings, and arrived in the 21st century as an outmoded, old-fashioned, judgemental word strongly associated with repressive religion. And it has itself been abused by the church, which throughout its history has publicly and privately pronounced individuals or actions sinful in very unhelpful ways. Today, we probably only ever use it or hear it flippantly – 'a sinful amount of chocolate'.

But in all this exploration, we are trying to unearth what sin really means, which at its heart is probably selfishness as opposed to 'otherishness'. It was Adam and Eve's helpless captivity to their desires for themselves and their benefit that unravelled the garden of Eden. This is why the human race can be said to be in need of saving. We need to be saved from ourselves, because we just can't save ourselves from our own impulses, as Paul so cogently expresses. And in order to retrieve the life that was lost in the garden of Eden, a life has to be given. If Jesus had not given his life for all humankind, the human race would have self-destructed, because of our bent for sin. Humankind is like a toddler obliviously chasing a ball into the path of an oncoming car. Unless the parent throws themself under the car and gives their life for the child, the toddler is lost.

History is full of real stories that capture some of the profundity of this and are an echo of Jesus' gift. One of them took place in 2018. Arnaud Beltrame, a French police officer, consciously and deliberately gave his life to save someone else. He knew that the result of his choice to take the place of the hostage was likely to mean his death. 'I think that Lieutenant Colonel Beltrame did what he did because of the specifically Christian saying, "Greater love hath no man than this, that a man lay down his life for his friends"… for Arnaud Beltrame had come, quite recently, to embrace Christianity. In aggressively secular, hard-boiled France, this must have been difficult to do.'[25]

> He is seated at the right hand of the father
> And he will come to judge the living and the dead.

Throughout history, injustice has always been met with the demand for justice and retribution for those responsible. Many examples come to mind, from those called to account for crimes of war or for abuse to specific events, such as the terrible Grenfell Tower fire of 2017 in London or various terrorist attacks across Europe. The world has always accepted appropriate punishment for wrongdoing. We are glad when those who have caused pain or abused their position of power, whether dictator, teacher or surgeon, are held to account.

At the same time, the concept of a God who pronounces judgement, whether for good or ill, has always caused tremendous theological indigestion. And it can cause real fear. A conversation between one of our grandchildren and his grandpa once turned to the fact that one day the world will wind up. This small boy became quite scared at this completely new idea, and Grandpa was roundly ticked off by his mum for frightening him.

Judgement is a heavy subject and complicated to talk about to anyone, let alone children, so perhaps the best angle to take is that of everything being made right and fair in the end by God, who is the most trustworthy judge of all. As Mr Beaver says in *The Lion, the Witch and the Wardrobe*, 'Wrong will be made right when Aslan comes in sight.'[26] At the end of time as we know it:

> God's dwelling-place is now among the people, and he will dwell with them... 'He will wipe every tear from their eyes. There will be no more death' or mourning or crying or pain, for the old order of things has passed away.[27]

Judgement is not Jesus' only occupation after his ascension; the writer of Hebrews tells us that he also 'always lives to intercede' at the right hand of the Father, to pray for us.[28] The ascended Lord takes up the role of permanent 'pray-er'. Think of it! We pray for each other sporadically. But for Jesus, this is a full-time role. There is never a moment or minute when you are not being prayed for. What is there not to like about this for a grandchild, who may have struggles at school or at home?

I believe in the Holy Spirit.

'In the beginning... the Spirit of God was hovering over the waters.'[29] I love this picture of the eternal brooding Holy Spirit, third person of the triune God. The Holy Spirit's omnipresence is our comfort and reassurance, and we can say with David, 'Where can I go from your Spirit?'[30] As well as being with us 24/7, he will fill us and be in us; he will teach us all things and make us holy, which has to do with our gradual transformation into the likeness of Jesus.[31] If only we could grasp the enormity of all this, we'd be so full of gratitude. Jesus' promise to his disciples that the gift of the Holy Spirit would be given to them, with the power to 'be my witnesses in Jerusalem, and in all Judea and Samaria, and to the ends of the earth',[32] speaks not of an oppressive or controlling power, but a winsome boldness to speak about the risen Christ.

This extraordinary promise was dramatically fulfilled on the day of Pentecost, as the Holy Spirit filled the hitherto terrified disciples with such courage that Peter preached with compelling power to the international crowd gathered in Jerusalem, and all the disciples found themselves understanding and speaking in languages they'd never been taught. Thousands were converted.[33]

Thousands! We can become so familiar with these remarkable biblical events that they cease to amaze us – but we should be amazed. Take a few minutes now to ponder on this history-changing day. Imagine what it might have felt like to be there. The Holy Spirit also gives us 'power, love and self-discipline'.[34] His power energises us to speak of Jesus, but he also gives us self-discipline so that we can bear his fruits. Year by year, he builds us up in kindness and gentleness of character and gives us vision and power, including for our old age, to influence and shape the next generations, especially through our prayers.

How we need the Holy Spirit as grandparents! Let's admit it, we can get a bit tired in the company of small children. Encountering the Holy Spirit, who is the spirit of Jesus, is an experience – an experience of God's love for you. Often people talk about being covered with a blanket of love, feeling themselves overwhelmed by liquid love. If we know this we can say with the apostle Paul, 'The Son of God… loved me and gave himself for me.'[35]

One of my earliest and most powerful experiences of the Holy Spirit came while listening to Handel's *Messiah*. It is said that when asked what his feelings were in writing the 'Hallelujah' chorus, Handel replied, 'I did think I did see all heaven before me, and the great God himself.' I was alone and listening to the words with a new attentiveness following the previous experience of the presence of God filling my little student room a year or so earlier:

> He was despised and rejected of men; a man of sorrows, and acquainted with grief… Surely, he hath borne our griefs, and carried our sorrows. He was wounded for our transgressions, he was bruised for our iniquities: the chastisement of our peace was upon him.[36]

Suddenly I was on the floor and a torrent of worship poured out of me as these words impacted me – he had died for me too. And then I exhausted all available superlatives and began to frame unknown words, what some have called the language of angels. To this day this language helps me pray when I don't know how to, and to lavish adoration upon God.

This is not something for adults only; the prophet Joel says, 'I will pour out my Spirit on all people… sons and daughters… old… young'.[37] Indeed, children may be naturally less self-conscious and more fascinated than adults by this kind of personal story, and indeed by the whole subject of prophecy, if handled with intelligence and care. They are, after all, used to the languages found in the writings of Tolkien, Philip Pullman and J.K. Rowling.

I believe in the holy catholic church, the communion of saints.

In chapter 8, 'The body beautiful', I explain why I believe in the church, so I will just say here that this statement underlines the longing of both God and humankind for unity in the worldwide body of Christ – a high and challenging calling. Note that 'catholic' here means universal, through all the world. John 17 expresses God's heart for unity, the longing for the kind of interconnectedness and interdependence exemplified in the Trinity: 'Protect them… so that they may be one as we are one.'[38] Where principle comes before the person, and conviction before compassion, we find competition instead of complementarity, and lose the beautiful aroma of unity, as expressed in Psalm 133.

I believe in the forgiveness of sins.

When I think of the thousands of mistakes I've made, the unkind things I've said in anger and the unfair ways I have treated my own children as they grew up – and I'm sure there is much more that I am blind to (as King David says, 'See if there is any offensive way in me'[39]) – it's an overwhelming relief to know that real forgiveness is possible; that is, forgiveness that doesn't leave the aftertaste of guilt, that is unconditional.

There is, however, a corollary: if we can receive this, we must also give it. Learning to forgive is difficult, especially in cases of serious and long-lasting damage. But to forgive is not to say no wrong has been done; rather it is to forgo any shred of retribution. To forgive is to let go, to let God bring justice. This will surely be a subject of significance for our grandchildren, who are growing up in a culture that emphasises blame and unforgiveness, because it's hard to see or understand alternatives when we are embedded in cultural norms.

I believe in the resurrection of the body and the life everlasting.

What an upbeat place to end! A friend who is exploring Christianity with some seriousness following a health scare reminded me that as grandparents we are nearer to death and the end of our lives on earth and so might have some wisdom to offer on the subject. We are no longer under the illusion that we can save or transform the world, and the bits of our bodies that are probably beginning to weaken or wear out will reinforce this reality. With imagination, we can tell them about the wonder of Jesus surprising the disciples with his reappearance – about how he had a new body of a different order. While he could cook and eat – Jesus made breakfast for his disciples – he could also seemingly walk through walls – he appeared among his disciples even though they were in a house with the doors locked.[40] Our grandchildren have seen impossible things happen in the computer and console games they play and in the films they watch, but they know such things are fantasy. How much fun would it be to tell them about some *impossible* things that really *did* happen, and really will happen?

Most children first encounter death with the demise of a pet, and even that is shocking and traumatic, not because they don't know that animals and people die, but because it has come so close for the first time. In the pet annals of our family, Tilly, one of our grandchildren's four guinea pigs, came to a tragic end in their pond. With great creativity (and illegality) the children's parents put the corpse, a spade and their children into the car, drove to the local cemetery and conducted a fitting burial service, complete with eulogy. Thank goodness no one saw them!

But for some the trauma is on another scale when a parent or grandparent dies. How comforting would it be to reassure them that they will see Grandma, Gramps, Mummy or Daddy again?

Paul describes this at some length in his letter to the Corinthians, ending his argument like this:

> In the resurrection scheme of things, this has to happen: everything perishable taken off the shelves and replaced by the imperishable, this mortal replaced by the immortal. Then the saying will come true: Death swallowed by triumphant Life! Who got the last word, oh, Death? Oh, Death, who's afraid of you now?[41]

This is a good moment to consider the strength of our certainty that heaven is real. It's something we know by faith, especially when a person dies. While writing this book, two young women I knew and loved died after terrible battles with cancer, aged 29 and 34. The ensuing painful grief reawakened the loss of another young friend several years ago, crushed to death by a cement lorry in a hideous cycling accident. She was 34 too. There's no answer to 'Why?', but I think there's an answer to 'What now?' C.S. Lewis expresses it like this:

> When we see the face of God we shall know that we have always known it… in heaven there will be no anguish and no duty of turning away from our earthly Beloveds. First because we shall have turned already; from the portraits to the original,

from the rivulets to the Fountain, from the creatures he made loveable to Love Himself. But secondly because we shall find them all in Him.[42]

You may be asking, 'Are you explaining all this stuff to a five-year-old or a 15-year-old?' The answer is neither at the moment. I'm just thinking through the bare bones of my faith with you. Philosophers and theologians have grappled with these concepts for centuries and come up with a myriad of ways in which to understand the nature of God and explain the tenets of Christianity. How I try to answer a question I'm lucky enough to be asked about any of the 'bare bones' will depend upon the age of the questioner. My first goal is to remind myself of these deep truths of the ancient future: this creed that will hold steady till the end of time, and to which followers of Jesus can hold on through the shifting cultural sands of their season. At the same time, I accept the limitations of my understanding. I know that I still see through a glass darkly, but I want to draw upon the wisdom of the ages and sages to help me.

Timothy Keller compares Christianity with the great fairy tales and legends, which:

> did not really happen... And yet they seem to fulfil a set of longings in the human heart that realistic fiction can never touch or satisfy. That is because deep in the human heart there are these desires – to experience the supernatural, to escape death, to know love that we can never lose, to not age but live long enough to realise our creative dream... to triumph over evil... Our hearts long for these things, and a well-told story momentarily satisfies these desires, scratching the terrible itch...
>
> Then we come to the Christmas story... At first glance it looks like the other legends. Here is a story about someone from a different world who breaks into ours and has miraculous powers and can calm the storm and heal people and raise

people from the dead. Then his enemies turn on him, and he is put to death, and it seems like all hope is over, but finally he rises from the dead and saves everyone.[43]

This, says Keller, is the 'true myth', the one all the others are feeling for, the one that really is factually true.

So where have we got to? Weaving through the huge tenets of my creed – incarnation, sacrifice, salvation, resurrection, the uniqueness of Jesus – I find myself surprised again by joy, the joy of the faith I long ago discovered – or rather that discovered me. I find hope springing up again that I may also have the joy of conversations with my grandchildren about this creed. What I long for most is that my grandchildren might know that it's all about Jesus – that friendship with God through Jesus is possible, and that this is the most wonderful and exciting thing we could hope for. I long that they might meet him for themselves. Ever since my dramatic encounter with God's presence as a student, the greatest constant has been the conviction that, where faith is concerned, Jesus is the one who stands alone. He is unique. Still to this day he makes ever more sense to me as God in human form than any other attempt to justify or explain God's relation to humans – God making himself nothing, as Paul's letter to the Philippians says, and becoming a servant; God taking the initiative to translate himself so that we, his creatures, could understand him.

How I pray it may be so for you and your grandchildren, and for me and mine.

6

Books and the book of books

Defend the Bible? I'd rather defend a lion.

Charles Haddon Spurgeon[1]

You Christians look after a document containing enough dynamite to blow all civilisation to pieces, turn the world upside down and bring peace to a battle-torn planet. But you treat it as though it is nothing more than a piece of literature.

Mahatma Gandhi[2]

In 2017, the Museum of the Bible was opened in Washington, DC. Whatever one might think of it, the museum is an astonishing feat of engineering and creativity. It charts the history, narrative and impact of the Bible through the ages, and its stated intention is to 'invite all people to engage with the Bible'. At the entrance you are greeted by 40-foot bronze doors with panels carrying the first verse of Psalm 19 in multiple languages: 'The heavens declare the glory of God; the skies proclaim the work of his hands.'[3] These are immediately awe-inspiring, yet walking into the grand lobby, the impact of its dimensions and the digital display on the ceiling that rotates through colourful designs throughout the day is overwhelming.

I wondered why I felt tears welling up within the first few seconds. Perhaps it was a mixture of relief and hope – relief that this beloved book, so despised and deconstructed, and often dust-laden, had appeared robed in glory and standing tall, so to speak, dressed in the most fantastic apparel; and hope that because of being opened, explored and celebrated on such an immense scale, it might bring hope to thousands of people from all nations, in a new revelatory way. Interestingly, the president of the museum at the time of our visit said that people of all faiths and none were streaming into the museum, and that when asked for feedback about what had impacted them most, the overwhelming response was that it gave them hope. 'People are not looking for history; they're looking for hope,' he said.

Needless to say, there has been no shortage of contestation over the Museum of the Bible, but we should not expect otherwise where this controversial and challenging book is concerned. The Bible is huge, written by over 30 authors across approximately 1,400 years. This fact alone means that it's complicated, and therefore it unsurprisingly seems contradictory in some places and unreasonably demanding in others. Of course, it's difficult to understand. Why would we expect otherwise? God is not a puppetmaster, so the Bible is not a rule book. Created in his image as we are, we have and must exercise freedom of choice as we seek to understand God's book. That it's possible to misunderstand and misuse it is, therefore, self-evident.

However, in this chapter, I wish to approach the Bible as the love letter it has become to me over the years. We might also remember and be encouraged by the fact that with estimated total sales of over five billion copies, the Bible is widely considered to be the bestselling book of all time. It sells approximately 100 million copies annually and has been arguably the major influence on literature and history throughout the world, especially in the west.

There are lots of reasons why the Bible is so provocative. One is that it relentlessly points to Jesus as the unique expression of God. Jesus himself confirms this, when he says, 'You study the Scriptures diligently because you think that in them you have eternal life. These are the very Scriptures that testify about me.'[4] Juliet reflects:

As far as the Bible is concerned, I always tell my grandchildren to use their brains and look for the deeper truth. What is *really* being said here, and what did it mean for the people of the time, and what is this passage saying to them today? I tell them that if it is just a handbook about what to do and what not to do, then it fails miserably. It is far more important than that. It is a way of being and in it we can find peace in the chaos and shelter in the storm. And if they read the life of Jesus, they will come across the greatest radical ever! If they want to be unconventional and reject the establishment, then read the life of Jesus. The incarnation and resurrection, what he said and the way he lived his life are the most important facts and things about him.

Another reason is that it challenges our independent spirit and our pride. Mark Twain was no theologian, but he had a certain earthy wisdom. He reportedly said, 'It ain't the parts of the Bible that I can't understand that bother me; it's the parts that I do understand.' In the same vein, Kierkegaard wrote:

> The Bible is very easy to understand. But we Christians are a bunch of scheming swindlers. We pretend to be unable to understand it because we know very well that the minute we understand, we are obliged to act accordingly.

Before we look at some of the motley crew that make up the Bible's grandparents, there's a prior question to be answered: why should we look to the Bible for prototypes and patterns, for alerts and advice, in the first place? My task in this book is not to be an apologist for the Bible; many others have expertly and convincingly done this.[5] But I hold a high view of the Bible; in fact, I really love the Bible. I believe it is God's permanent and definitive message to humanity.

'The Holy Scriptures are our letter from home,' said Augustine of Hippo. The apostle Paul, writing to his protégé Timothy, says of the Bible:

All Scripture is God-breathed and is useful for teaching, rebuking, correcting and training in righteousness, so that the servant of God may be thoroughly equipped for every good work.[6]

Peter, the apostle who probably underwent the most radical conversion apart from Paul, writes in his second letter:

Above all, you must understand that no prophecy of Scripture came about by the prophet's own interpretation of things. For prophecy never had its origin in the human will, but prophets, though human, spoke from God as they were carried along by the Holy Spirit.[7]

Scholars and theologians – of which I am grateful to be neither – have wrestled though the centuries with the questions raised by this unique book.

My purpose here as one who agrees with the self-assessment in its pages is to glean wisdom for us as grandparents. I often liken it to a large jigsaw. I don't really like jigsaws, which usually have large tracts of sky or landscape that involve connecting thousands of seemingly identical pieces, and I have neither the devotion nor the patience for such a frustrating task. However, my own laziness in this regard illustrates for me the complexity of getting to grips with the Bible. At first sight there are things that jar and offend, particularly in the Old Testament, and there are also apparent contradictions scattered throughout the Bible's pages. Like a huge puzzle, it can feel like way too much effort to try to arrange the pieces in ways that both make sense and feed our souls. The great 19th-century preacher Charles Spurgeon expresses this in florid language:

There are times when solitude is better than society, and silence is wiser than speech. We should be better Christians if we were more alone, waiting upon God, and gathering through meditation on His Word spiritual strength for labour in his service. We ought to muse upon the things of God, because we thus get the real nutriment out of them… Why is it that some Christians, although they hear many sermons, make but slow advances in the divine life? Because they neglect their closets, and do not thoughtfully meditate on God's Word. They love the wheat, but they do not grind it; they would have the corn, but they will not go forth into the fields to gather it; the fruit hangs upon the tree, but they will not pluck it; the water flows at their feet, but they will not stoop to drink it.[8]

It's all too easy to defend like tigers our opinions or points of views, but when made aware of other factors, we may see things differently. When churches and denominations conduct vociferous theological arguments in public, it is a travesty of Jesus' prayer and teaching in John 17; and it often comes about through focusing on particular texts or doctrines at the expense of the whole. In the same way that distance grants a more comprehensive view – think of an astronaut seeing the earth from the moon – determining to familiarise ourselves with the whole Bible, including the boring and obscure bits, will give us increased understanding as well as keeping us humbly aware that this book is bigger and deeper than us. Like a large puzzle, we may only add one small piece at a time, but the whole is there on the lid of the box to refer to as we progress.

Many astronauts, those few members of the human race who have had the opportunity and courage to travel into space, have been rewarded with profound revelations about human existence. Apollo 14 astronaut Edgar Mitchell said, 'From out there on the moon, international politics look so petty. You want to grab a politician by the scruff of the neck and drag him a quarter of a million miles out and say, "Look at that!"' Perspective realises an anger and a frustration, which is echoed by many astronauts. Other comments from astronauts have become immortalised: 'I didn't feel like a giant. I felt very, very small' (Neil Armstrong in 1969); 'When I first looked back at the earth, standing on the moon, I cried' (Alan Shepard, 1971).

Others have commented in the same vein from the much safer location of a writer's desk. Carl Sagan describes the 'Pale Blue Dot' image of the earth taken by *Voyager 1* six billion kilometres away in 1990, saying, 'There is perhaps no better a demonstration of the folly of human conceits than this distant image of our tiny world.'[9] Perhaps we might say of the Bible, 'There is perhaps no better a demonstration of the folly of personalised theology than opening oneself to the perspective afforded by surveying the glorious panorama of the whole Bible.'

These thoughts capture something of wonder, humility, holiness and even mystery, and they are a perfect illustration of how our approach to the Bible might change were we to view the whole rather than fixating on the parts. It is all too easy to use the Bible for our own ends, perhaps building an argument for or against something, with selective texts. Were we to expand our vision, taking in the wider view, with all its mysteries that elude our understanding, we might gain some understanding that would make us a little more like Jesus. As Dwight L. Moody, American evangelist and publisher connected with the Holiness Movement, said, 'The Bible was not given for our information but for our transformation.'

Another astronaut, Roger Chaffee, said, 'The world itself looks cleaner and so much more beautiful. Maybe we can make it that way – the way God intended it – by giving everybody that new perspective from out in space.' Chaffee never realised this dream, for he lost his life in a fire during a pre-launch test in 1967, but he'd seen images from earlier space missions, and he had a vision.

This can speak to us as Christian grandparents. We have a vision too – we dream of being able to somehow communicate a vision of the Bible that's like the vision of the world that astronauts see. We may not wholly realise our dream, but we can pursue it by being men and women who love the whole Bible without claiming to understand it all. We can choose to regard it as more powerful and durable than ourselves. We can choose to respect it rather than criticise or ridicule it. We can tell our grandchildren that we treasure it and believe it contains deeper wisdom than the changing values of culture and civilisation.

'Open my eyes that I may see wonderful things in your law.'[10] This is the approach to the Bible that I want to share with my grandchildren. I see these words on my cupboard door every day: 'Your statutes are my delight; they are my counsellors.'[11]

It's against the vast background of the Bible as a whole world to discover that we'll home in on a few of the Bible's grandparents. Needless to say, we'll find some don'ts as well as some dos. The Bible contains more X-rated material than any movie; it does not shy away from violence, horror or pornography. Jesus said, 'There is nothing concealed that will not be disclosed, or hidden that will not be made known,'[12] so no act committed by humanity is a surprise or shock to God. 'Nothing in all creation is hidden from God's sight. Everything is uncovered and laid bare before the eyes of him to whom we must give account.'[13]

Choice is always before us, and God has provided a handbook to help us make good ones, in which he shows the consequences of different choices we can and will make. One of the things that sets the Bible apart from all other literature is that it claims to be alive – not usually a word used to describe a book: 'The word of God is alive and active. Sharper than any double-edged sword, it penetrates even to dividing soul and spirit… it judges the thoughts and attitudes of the heart.'[14]

This means that it will reveal different things to different people, and different things to the same person at different times. I don't mean contradictory things, but rather that revelation will be progressive, in the sense of becoming slowly fuller, more properly grasped and understood.

Before we put individual characters under the microscope, let me illustrate what I mean from the life of Abraham, in Genesis 22, where we find the strange story of a loving God apparently asking Abraham to sacrifice the precious son he had waited decades for. To a child, the Genesis 22 story looks as if it really is the horrifying tale of a man prepared to kill his own son – definitely not Sunday-school material, at least not if you don't want your child to subconsciously register God as an irrational axe murderer. Perhaps as an adolescent it seems completely contradictory – there's Abraham, who's waited a long time for this child, with whose birth have come promises about the future of his people, and suddenly he's tying him up on a home-made altar and holding some kind of machete over him.

More time passes, and as a young professional, now a Christian, I realise that child sacrifice was relatively common in the Canaanite cultures, so God's intervention in that context was a huge act of grace. Years pass again, and now I have a baby, and I'm looking at the story from another angle. Nothing compares with the fierce love I have for my own child; I would give up my life for them. Now, thousands of years and miles distant from Abraham, I see how God did not withhold his own son, and how when the moment of this crucifixion sacrifice came, there was no voice that said, 'Do not lay a hand on the boy... The Lord Will Provide.'[15] And I have a tiny glimpse of the suffering of God. And if I dwell here a moment, I can think myself into the pages – this page with the old father who had no idea where all this was going. Or did he? Easy to miss in the story is Abraham's comment as he instructs the servants to wait for them and look after the donkey: 'We will worship and then *we* will come back to you.'[16] Then on a much later page another son cries out, 'My God, my God, why have you forsaken me?'[17] And the pages start breathing and suddenly the words are alive, and some tears come because I don't know whether I love and trust God as much as Abraham. I want to, but I don't know.

You and I would love our grandchildren to treasure this living book as we do. How can we unwrap it for them in a way that makes this more likely? Clearly our choice of which stories to pick out matters. While most of us won't become theology experts, I want to encourage a dedication to the pursuit of understanding the Bible. Let's be unafraid of exploring things that are hard to understand and aspire to be able to answer questions knowing that often the answer will be, 'I don't really know, but these are my thoughts so far.'

One of my granddaughters recently asked me to read the Bible with her and asked for the story about Adam and Eve. I was so delighted and warmed by this sweet request, but took a deep breath as we started, because there's a wealth of possibilities for getting it wrong – for giving the impression that God is cruel and strange, and that he deliberately makes things difficult for Adam and Eve by placing a tree full of beautiful fruit seductively in the middle of the garden, and then telling them they can't eat any of the fruit. It's like holding out a bag of pick-and-mix at the cinema and saying, 'Look, but on no account touch, and certainly don't eat!' How likely are they to obey that? There is so much room here for developing a negative image of God, and many interpretations of the story that we call 'the fall' have made sin the main point.

But, as Danielle Shroyer points out in her book *Original Blessing: Putting sin in its rightful place*, there is more about blessing than sin in this story. There's more about God's kindness and care, his protection and love, than there is about his justice at this point. He has declared all that he has made to be 'very good'[18] and then places Adam in a gorgeous garden with all the food his heart can desire and provides him with a wife with whom he can enjoy all the delights of human companionship, including physical intimacy.

As if this weren't enough, God has created both Adam and Eve in his own image. Back here in Genesis the main thing we know about God is that he is the great creator. His creative powers are unlimited, as we have seen in the descriptions of the forming universe and in the even more astonishing fact that God creates just by speaking – he says, 'Let there be light', and there is light.[19] And he has decided to make man and woman in his own image,[20] which means that they are going to be super-creative, too. There's so much in Genesis that is amazing to talk about with children, so much that is positive and mind-blowing, yet so often we carry into adulthood a negative view of the story.

It's worth saying here that how we talk about sexual intimacy entirely depends upon the age of the child. If we are fortunate enough to ever find ourselves discussing Genesis with a grandchild, it is naturally our job to make our discussion age-appropriate. It's also worth reminding ourselves that a major cultural shift since many of us were children is the disappearance of the taboo around sex and sexuality. Teenagers and young adults are far more comfortable talking about sex and employing terminology that might have made us squeamish in our youth. How this has come about – developments in technology, the advent of the internet and social media, the relentless pushing back of boundaries around sexuality and ethics – is not all bad, but we had better be ready to find ourselves in some potentially quite blunt conversations.

Returning to Adam and Eve, let's look at some of the questions that naturally arise. Why on earth were they wearing no clothes? Weren't they embarrassed? Or cold? Here's the opportunity (tailored to the age of the child, of course) to think about things or situations that make us feel ashamed or embarrassed, things that make us wish we were different. It could be a chance to find out a bit more about their real feelings about school; it may even be that difficult things about home emerge. When we are naked, we feel vulnerable, exposed and threatened. That's obvious even to the smallest child, if we are talking literally about the body. But what about feeling we have no clothes covering the invisible parts of us – our mind, soul or emotions? Even small children can feel afraid, silly or embarrassed. The point about Adam and Eve being naked here is that they were completely secure because their creator and Father was with them, loving them and keeping them safe. Nothing could harm them as long as this was true.

'So why,' asks your grandchild, 'did they listen to the serpent and eat the fruit?' (By the way, the word 'apple' doesn't appear in the biblical text.) Good question, and a good opportunity to talk about the power of temptation – that overwhelming longing that makes you, *makes* you, sneak a few sweets out of the tin; or, for older children getting to grips with the internet, that powerful desire that creates the urge to buy something that promises strength, beauty, intelligence, pleasure or knowledge: whatever form of power the flashing advert promises. The serpent tells them they will be like God, and so much unhappiness is caused by the simple but sinister desire to be like someone else. Who does your grandchild want to be like, and why? This could be a good moment to talk about their careful creation and their uniqueness: 'For you created my inmost being; you knit me together in my mother's womb.'[21] That could be a new thought for a child, along with the next couple of verses, which evoke the slow and meticulous growth of the baby through the nine months. Many children now are familiar with an ultrasound scan photo of a sibling, and combining the benefits of such medical technology with the idea that God is involved in 'weaving us together' as our life comes into being could be both surprising and comforting for a child.

My purpose here is simply to illustrate the endless possibilities of discussion and faith-building that can come from exploring the Bible with our grandchildren. Equally, it's a plea that we as Christian grandparents take seriously our own responsibility to aspire to be Bible adepts, always learning more from writers, preachers, theologians and friends. Let's tell stories about the Bible that make it a 'now' book and that fascinate our grandchildren, such as the story of the first missionary to Korea, who was martyred by the very man he handed a Bible to as he landed on the country's shore; legend has it that the pages of that Bible were used to wallpaper the same man's house, which led to the conversion of many and the establishment of the first church in that nation.[22]

Fortunately, we're far from alone in this calling to bring the Bible to life. Today there are plenty of apps and DVD series, such as *VeggieTales* for little ones, which connect Bible stories with the world we and our grandchildren inhabit. There are camps, holiday clubs and annual conferences, such as New Wine, Spring Harvest, Focus and Keswick, all of which have well-established children's programmes of the highest quality. There are also multiple presentations of the Bible for young people, and a plethora of versions for children, as well as numerous storybooks that highlight one event or another.

That said, not everyone agrees that they are a help. Juliet says:

> I'm afraid we have never given our grandchildren storybooks from the Bible… I don't think that learning the 'stories' is a good way into faith. I think it can put off a child, because they come to think of Christianity as just another story from an illustrated storybook. I would much rather get them to read a modern translation of the Bible when they are teenagers. I think they are much more likely to respect what they find inside and to use their brains to see what the story is really about.

It's a good point. We want to avoid our grandchildren coming to think of the life of Jesus as just another story. If we do give Bible storybooks, it's a pertinent reminder that we are then responsible for helping our grandchild understand that the books are just that – storybooks – illustrations of a much bigger and true story.

Hopefully by now we are encouraged to revitalise our own familiarity with the Bible, if need be, and encouraged that there is plenty out there to help us introduce our grandchildren to it. Let's brush the dust off the Bible, reminded that it's filled from end to end with adventure, and vibrant with the life it claims to have. Let's be confident that it's trustworthy and true despite the complexities.

And remember, as Billy Graham said, 'I've read the last page of the Bible and it's all going to turn out all right.'

7

Wonderful and terrible: the Bible's grandparents

Then Israel said, 'Bring them to me so I may bless them.'
GENESIS 48:9

[Jeroboam] did evil in the eyes of the Lord.
2 KINGS 14:24

Having zoomed out to consider the whole Bible, and the vast breadth of creation and humanity that it covers, let's zoom in and place a few grandparents under the microscope and see what we as grandparents today might learn from them.

The patriarchs are the most obvious examples of grandparents in the Bible. Although we're not told how they measured up in the eyes of their grandchildren, in the context of the oral culture in which they lived, people will certainly have been familiar with their grandparents and their exploits.

There are plenty of grandparents to choose from – Adam, Eve, Noah, Adah, Zillah and so on – and like us they are both inspirational and deeply disappointing in equal measure. We'll look fair and square at both aspects, but we'll start upbeat with what inspires, and with Abraham, one of the most fully developed characters in the Bible.

Abraham was first a man of faith, prepared to follow God without really knowing why or where. Hebrews 11 gives a lot of space to Abraham, speaking repeatedly of his faith. He 'made his home in the promised land like a stranger in a foreign country'.[1] He believed against all odds – his age (99) and Sarah's infertility – that God was able to give him a child. In the bizarre story of Genesis 22, which we looked at in the previous chapter, in which God tests Abraham by asking him to sacrifice his long-awaited precious son, we see that God means more to Abraham than anything else, including Isaac.

Abraham had great faith. What is faith? 'Faith is confidence in what we hope for and assurance about what we do not see.'[2] Abraham couldn't see at all where this was going, but he plodded on up the mountain, sure that somehow he could trust God.

This doesn't mean that we'll receive all we hope for in this life. In this same chapter of Hebrews, we read that, among others, Abraham 'did not receive the things promised; [he] only saw them and welcomed them from a distance'.[3] He did receive some things, namely Isaac; the verse refers to the inheritance of the land that God had promised him.[4]

Faith is a beautiful thing. One of my daughters once gave me a card on which was printed, 'The best things in life aren't things.' I read it often. One of the best things in life is faith, which delivers us from the many seductions of this world and can make a person truly free. Faith assures us that our existence is much bigger than that which the naked eye perceives, and it enables us to hold on in times of trial or tragedy. It was faith that helped me hold on after the death of our first son in a cot death. I believed then, as I do now, that he is alive in heaven and that I will see him again. As King David said of his deceased infant son, 'I will go to him, but he will not return to me.'[5] We expressed this faith for ourselves by inscribing our baby's gravestone with the words, 'Samuel grew up in the presence of the Lord.'[6] If I can communicate the beauties of faith to my grandchildren, even in small measure, I will be grateful and blessed – makarios, to use the Greek word; that is, happy in the deeper, wider sense of the word, a happiness that comes from peace and contentment, not circumstances. This is a lovely idea, but what does it mean in practice? It means demonstrating that I don't live for acquisition and pleasure. 'Easy,' you might think, but since so much of children's lives revolves around food, activity and, yes, acquisition, it means thinking before spending.

Abraham was wonderfully generous and open-handed. We see this in his relationship with his nephew Lot. 'Abram had become very wealthy in livestock and in silver and gold.'[7] He was indeed makarios. But the expansion of his wealth and possessions had one adverse consequence, which was that the land could no longer support both his and the next generation's livestock. With wisdom, Abraham offered Lot the choice of which part of the land to opt for, since, as he pointed out, the whole land was due to be theirs. Lot chose what he thought would bring him the greatest profit – his thought was for himself rather than Abraham. As the story unfolds we see that generosity brings its own rewards, both in being protected from loss, and more importantly in a reaffirmation of God's covenant promise of the land to his descendants.

Abraham's generosity is further seen in the story of the purchase of his burial site after Sarah's death from Ephron the Hittite. Ephron offered the site as a gift,[8] and his words convey something of the respect and honour in which Abraham was by now held as an elderly and dignified figure. While there is nothing inherently wrong in either giving or receiving a gift, there was a sense of integrity and righteousness at play here, as Abraham insisted on paying for the site.

I pray that my grandchildren will experience us as generous people, not just with money, but with our time and our attention. I'd love to have listened to the conversation Abraham had with his family about this purchase. 'Dad, Grandpa, why on earth didn't you just accept the gift?' What would he have answered? I suspect that the encounter also reflected Abraham's political savvy; he was shrewd enough to avoid becoming beholden to the Hittites, who would later become adversaries of the Israelites. Maybe he didn't want to leave any potential bargaining chip on the table, and perhaps this was part of what he told his family.

Abraham is a towering figure in the Bible, but he was also flawed, and while such characters are enshrined to inspire us, they are also there to warn us. What disappoints about this patriarch?

It's so tempting to help God answer our prayers. Our minds work feverishly to give him the leads he needs, and this is exactly what Abraham did – or rather what Sarah suggested he do. Together they engineered early surrogacy, as Abraham capitulated to what must have looked like a brilliant idea, particularly as it was suggested by his wife, so she couldn't really complain or be jealous. Or could she? Desire is a powerful and often cruel master, and when it grows strong in us we easily throw caution and wisdom to the wind, and make choices or promises, or in this case love (maybe more business-like than romantic or erotic), that have far-reaching and catastrophic consequences. None of these things can be unmade, and in this case getting the longed-for child brought not joy but heartache and division. Hagar was banished, Abraham and Sarah's marriage was soured, and Sarah and Hagar fell out with each other. Incidentally this very story gives a crucial insight into the effects of sex without boundaries and is a warning to us to resist the power of temptation. James writes, 'Each person is tempted when they are dragged away by their own evil desire and enticed. Then, after desire has conceived, it gives birth to sin; and sin, when it is full-grown, gives birth to death.'[9]

Lifelong hostility between Isaac and Ishmael was the fruit of this engineered fulfilment of God's promise. The angel of the Lord, while comforting the beleaguered Hagar, tells her that her son will be wild: 'His hand will be against everyone and everyone's hand against him, and he will live in hostility towards all his brothers.'[10]

Another aspect of this story is that it calls us to be our own person, and not to be over-influenced by others. This is much more difficult when it concerns those close to us, and when the line between being persuaded against our better judgement and having the courage of our convictions is thin. The presence of a strong desire makes the line wobbly as well as thin. But God calls us to make him our first line of enquiry: '[David] enquired of the Lord.'[11] Abraham should have said, 'Wait, let's ask God.' But who are we to pass judgement? Here was a husband and wife, both growing older and past the glory days of sexual union, not least because of perpetual disappointment. Here was a man presented with an invitation to sexual intimacy with a much younger woman by the very person to whom he has been faithful for long, childless decades. How seductive! How confusing! It must have really done his head in.

One final warning from the life of Abraham. He lied. As he arrived in the Negev region and engaged with the residents, he introduced Sarah as his sister. King Abimelek somehow encountered her and took a fancy to her. We've noted already Sarah's age – 'Abraham and Sarah were already very old, and Sarah was past the age of childbearing'[12] – but she obviously held some attraction for Abimelek.

Lying, of course, leaves a trail of destruction behind it and a web into which many become ensnared as their story collapses, often on a technicality. The prohibition against lying is enshrined in the ninth commandment, 'You shall not give false testimony against your neighbour.'[13] In Abraham's mind this was a white lie, a half-truth, as he and Sarah were actually related. But he omitted their more significant relationship, their marriage, opening the way to serious consequences, in this case infertility across Abimelek's entire household.

Living as we do in an age of post-truth, where what I feel can take precedence over fact, our grandchildren are unlikely to be unaffected by the massaging of information. As Christian grandparents, we can adopt a hard line on truth-telling: not a hard attitude, just a clear distinction between truth and falsehood. Telling the truth can be costly, but we can hope that our grandchildren might witness us preferring truth to saving face or impressing someone.

Thanks to my parents, I grew up with a tender conscience and an almost reverence for the truth. To this day, I am something of a tiger for it. I demonstrated this at the age of eight, when I cheated in a test by peering over the shoulder of the girl in front of me to see the answer. Utterly convicted afterwards, I went to tell the head teacher, whose response was a gentle, 'Well done, Anita. Owning up is half the battle. Don't do it again, dear.' Extreme conscience, don't you think? Yes. But think how safe it feels to trust a person you know will always tell the truth, whatever the cost.

Many of the things we can draw from the character of Abraham can also be seen in the lives of other biblical grandparents. Not only does lying reap misery and conflict, but it breeds. Isaac also lied about his relationship to Rebekah to Abimelek, fearing that desire for his beautiful wife might lead to his death. Lies may conceal us temporarily but will always end by exposing us. The Bible tells us we can be sure our sin will find us out,[14] and our grandchildren are living through a time when the truth of this is being played out before the nation, as a stream of individuals is paraded in the media, found out and exposed for their crimes. Among them are such children's TV presenters as Jimmy Savile and Rolf Harris, who not only traumatised those they abused, but also broke the trust of thousands. Once betrayed, trust can take years to rebuild; sadly, sometimes its beyond recovery.

Like Sarah, Rebekah tried to help God fulfil his promises to her. Accustomed to prayer, she asked God about the twins she was carrying, but when she heard that the younger would serve the older, it set in motion a trail of family disaster and conflict. We travel through the story of Jacob,[15] the younger twin, stealing his father's blessing through deception – all masterminded by his mother, who was 'helping' God – into the resulting enmity between the brothers, an enmity so strong that Esau resolved to kill his brother. Rebekah then despatched Jacob to her brother Laban.

As lying breeds lying, so deception, which is a form of lying, breeds deception, and clearly this was a family trait, because the next example of it is Laban deceiving Jacob by giving him his daughter Leah in reward for his seven years' labour instead of her sister, Rachel, with whom Jacob was in love. As Jacob's family expanded over the years, he brought prosperity to Laban, but the tables were turned when Jacob deceived Laban by managing their joint livestock in favour of his own flocks, and then fleeing secretly with his now numerous livestock and family.

The deception/lying gene re-emerges in Rachel, who stole her father's household gods, hiding them inside her camel's saddlebag. When Laban caught up with the family, furious at not being kept informed and complaining because he'd had no opportunity to 'kiss my grandchildren and my daughters goodbye',[16] Rachel lied to save her skin. Asked about the household gods, Jacob, who didn't know of Rachel's theft, said that if anyone is found to have them they shall die. Rachel, sitting on the saddle bags, claimed to be unable to stand because she was having her period.[17] How inappropriate, and what a mess in this extended family.

The generational dysfunctions of the patriarchs and their families are sobering warnings of the follies of lying and deception, of sex without borders, and of self-seeking and greed. However, we should remember that one of the thickest threads that runs end to end through the Bible is that of redemption, and the chapters of Genesis are punctuated by God's repeated assurance that he is with these flawed human beings, will watch over them and will not leave them until he has fulfilled his promise – that they will not only inherit the land but fill it with their descendants.[18] While we're warned by the mess, we must be warmed by God the Father, who won't leave us either.

Jacob had two profound encounters with Yahweh, one in a dream at Bethel, when he had fled from Esau and was on his way to Laban, and the other in a kind of waking dream at Peniel, when he had fled from Laban and was on his way back to meet Esau, hoping for reconciliation after all the years that had passed.[19] This latter encounter is a strange experience of wrestling through the night with a human-angelic being, and emerging at sunrise with a new name, Israel, and a limp resulting from a hip injury sustained in the night. Israel means 'Let God prevail' or 'God contends', and both the new name and the new limp symbolise the transformation in Jacob's character, from a selfish and scheming person into someone humbled by his experience and dependent on God. This renewed character is reflected in the account of his reunion with Esau.[20]

Jacob's later years didn't get easier, as we are launched into the long story of Joseph,[21] following the reconciliation between Jacob and Esau, and Isaac's death. Jacob is a background character throughout, but there are things to learn from him.

A primary cause of all that befell Joseph was Jacob's favouritism, which he openly displayed. It would be naive not to recognise that we are unlikely to have an identical natural affinity with all our grandchildren. There is nothing wrong with this, and we have no need to feel guilty. All sorts of different values from different backgrounds and histories have necessarily blended into our grandchildren's generation, and we will feel more comfortable with some of these differences than others. But natural affinity is not the same as love. We're called to love and accept each one equally, and Jacob was foolish to give Joseph preferential treatment.

Later, we encounter Jacob arguing with his sons about whether they can take Benjamin down to Egypt with them. We follow Jacob through the stages of absolute refusal – he had already lost Joseph – to understanding and acceptance that he needs to let go and trust God. The discussion ends with Jacob praying for God's mercy on the family and coming to a place of submission: 'As for me, if I am bereaved, I am bereaved.'[22] This is the Jacob who stole his brother's blessing, who practised deceit and whose chief interest was himself for much of his early life. But it's also the Jacob whose encounter with God at Peniel changed everything, so it's a touching moment, prompting affection for this seasoned grandfather.

His prayer was finally answered with the safe return from Egypt of his beloved Benjamin, with the unbelievable news that his lost son Joseph was not only alive but the 'ruler of Egypt', who will care for the whole family through the famine. We can only imagine the overwhelming joy this old man experienced – what a tumult of emotions! He was stunned, he didn't believe, and then he was convinced. As if this bumper crop of news wasn't enough, Jacob has a last encounter with the living God, who affirms what's happening. God speaks to him in a vision at night and tells him not to be afraid of going down to Egypt because that is where God will fulfil the promise made years earlier to Jacob that 'a nation and a community of nations will come from you'.[23] Now God tells him, 'I will go down to Egypt with you, and I will surely bring you back again.'[24] Jacob must have wondered how the prophetic promise made all those years ago at Bethel could be fulfilled, but here at Beersheba the answer comes.

It's interesting to note that this communication from God as Jacob sets out for Egypt comes in the context of worship. We, too, can let our grandchildren observe that we are worshippers and that we are in conversation with God – that the God we worship still speaks today. One of the most tender scenes in the Bible depicts Jacob's reunion with his long-lost son: 'As soon as Joseph appeared before him, he threw his arms around his father and wept for a long time.'[25] When Joseph introduces his father to Pharaoh, we see a man into whom the vicissitudes of life have built great spiritual stature and resilience as he blesses Pharaoh with dignity and respect.

Our last sight of Jacob is with his sons gathered around him, giving each the prophetic blessing appropriate to him. Some of his pronouncements are difficult to describe as blessings, but each son's departing words from his father are deeply interwoven with his life. What we are to note here is the power of blessing. We too are called to be people who bless.

I've taken time over Abraham, Sarah and Jacob, but there are plenty of others who merit equal attention. Some of the Old Testament characters we know from the text became grandparents: Joseph, Moses, Samuel, David, Solomon, Naomi and Ruth. Others we may assume became grandparents: Caleb, Deborah, Esther, Ezra and Nehemiah, to name but a few. Each of them holds out wise advice for us, not just as grandparents but as people of integrity as well as flaws in their dealings. We can't fail to be moved by the scenes of reconciliation between Joseph and his brothers in Egypt, and the extravagant expression of emotion at the reunion. Joseph's attitude is a model for us of gracious forgiveness. He's a man with great self-awareness, a man in touch with his feelings. Moses is a man of prayer. Samuel is a man who listens to the Lord from his youth. David is a man after God's own heart; he is a man who worships, who knows how to truly confess his sins and ask for forgiveness. Solomon asks for wisdom when he could have asked for anything. Naomi devotes herself freely to her widowed daughter-in-law Ruth. Ruth likewise cares for her mother-in-law and is attractive to Boaz because of her integrity. Esther displays humility in seeking advice from her uncle Mordecai, wisdom in her dealings with Haman and courage in exposing his plot to destroy her people.

Other biblical grandparents provide a warning rather than a model. The litany of the kings of Israel and Judah, who all became grandparents, records a preponderance of those who 'did evil in the eyes of the Lord', reminding us that as parents we can do our best to ensure that our children 'walk in the ways of God', but that we can't make it happen. The story of Hezekiah recounts the life of a righteous and prayerful man, but his son Manasseh and his grandson Amon both 'did evil in the eyes of the Lord', practising idolatry and engaging in occultism.[26] We might imagine or identify with Hezekiah's sadness and disappointment, and at the same time be reminded that we are not our grandchildren's saviours; we are only their loving and prayerful grandparents.

The New Testament offers us fewer grandparents and less by way of flamboyant characters, but there is lots of treasure to be found all the same. Paul, writing to Timothy, remarks on his 'sincere faith', pointing out that his mother Eunice and grandmother Lois were also women of faith. We know that Timothy had been taught the scriptures by them from his infancy, and that one of the reasons he was secure in his faith was precisely because of their integrity and trustworthiness.[27]

I want to mention two other characters, one of whom was probably a grandparent, and the other of whom may well have been. Joseph and Mary meet them both when they come to present Jesus in the temple.

The first is Simeon, to whom God has spoken, revealing that he will see the Christ before he dies.[28] Jesus looks like any other baby, but when Simeon sees him God supernaturally enables him to see that the moment he has waited so long for is here, and he bursts into worship. His presence in the Bible communicates patience and prayer to us and encourages us to be alert to the Holy Spirit's voice, the voice that both reassures us and may give us a message to pass on or prophesy. Prophecy can be general or specific; here it is specific and overflows from Simeon's worship of God.

The second is Anna, who has been a widow for 77 years after a seven-year marriage and has chosen to devote herself to prayer and fasting in the temple. She provides a striking contrast with the widows described by Paul in his letters to Timothy and Titus, where he points out that some are drawn into gossip through not having enough to do, or choose to live for pleasure.[29]

Reading the stories of these giant Old Testament figures can be intimidating, despite the blatant evidence of their character weaknesses. It's as if we are somehow myopic, and only take in what huge characters they were, full of colour and drama and power, but are blind to their flaws. Equally, the spiritual, holy New Testament figures can easily intimidate us in a different way. We say to ourselves, 'I can never be like him or her.' No, we can't, and we are not supposed to be. They're there with all their victories and defeats, their successes and failures, for us to study and learn something from. God can speak to us through them, if we will listen. And by far the most important takeaway is God's repeated assurances to them all that he is with them, and always will be; that he is for them, through the good times and the bad, through the prodigal times and the times of his close presence. And he's with us too – and with our tribe.

Juliet, who for many years following her eldest child's divorce has given a lot of time to caring for the three children, says:

> I say to our oldest three grandchildren over and over again, 'Whatever you do and whatever happens, I will always love you and always welcome you and always listen to you. I will offer you advice if you ask, but only if you ask. I will love you forever without question, and I will do everything in my power to be there for you in any circumstance. And I will always believe in you… because in the end this is what Jesus will do.'

That says it in a nutshell.

8

The body beautiful

The Church is the Church only when it exists for others.
Dietrich Bonhoeffer[1]

[God's] intent was that now, through the church, the manifold wisdom of God should be made known to the rulers and authorities in the heavenly realms.
EPHESIANS 3:10

The most common biblical analogy for the church is the bride of Christ, which immediately conjures up a picture of beauty, grace, freshness and purity, along with hope, excitement and celebration. To be dressed as a bride is a transformative experience, beautifying the plainest of women. At weddings the guests always say to the bride, 'You look radiant, gorgeous, stunning.' In Ephesians 5, we read that husbands are to love their wives 'just as Christ loved the church and gave himself up for her to make her holy... radiant... without stain or wrinkles or any other blemish'.[2] I wish!

We are a corporate bride, called to gather as the people of God and be slowly transformed by the Spirit of God so that we become the bride that Christ loves and gave himself up for. The practice of church is also beautifully described in two passages in Acts. As the church was birthed, the new believers devoted themselves to the apostles' teaching and to each other, to the breaking of bread and to prayer. They saw wonders and signs; they shared everything and sold their goods to support each other as needs arose. They met together every day in the temple courts, and every day people came to faith in Jesus and joined them. 'All the believers were one in heart and mind.' They testified to the resurrection of the Lord with great power, and the community was full of grace. All needs were met and people even sold land and houses to do so, entrusting the money raised to the apostles to distribute.[3]

Today in the UK, we might be surprised to hear that the predominant religion in the world is Christianity, and that may be because in many ways Europe, where the gospel first came via Philippi, has become the dark continent, while people are streaming to Christ in other parts of the world, especially in Africa, Latin America and Asia. There are 2.3 billion Christians in the world, representing 38,000 denominations. While this tragically reflects division, it also reflects the glorious diversity of the people of God. It's a foretaste of every nation, people, tribe and tongue.

This is the kind of picture to share with grandchildren: people of all kinds, shapes, sizes, colours and convictions gathering around the person of Jesus Christ; the indescribable joy of worshipping him together; the pleasure of understanding more of the Bible through teaching, sermons and talks; the excitement of meeting people from all around the world, yet feeling that somehow we know them. They are familiar despite our differences because of Jesus. I want to share all sorts of experiences of church that I've had: sober liturgy and soaring choral song in the cathedral that my parents attended; exuberant celebration in an ordinary Sunday service; wild festive dancing and whooping that seemingly lasts for hours in west Africa; loud, long, impassioned prayer meetings in South Korea or east Africa; studying the Bible in small family-style groups and praying for each other as we share our sadness and admit our failures and needs. These are just a few faces of the multiracial, multi-ethnic, multilingual, multigenerational, utterly spectacular bride of Jesus Christ.

Even if our own experience of church has been limited and we haven't had the opportunity of travelling and meeting other styles of church, we're able to read of distant places and talk about them.

We can show and tell, as primary school children do. Whatever her shortcomings, the bride of Christ is on her way to radiance and is beautiful to behold. 'I will build my church, and the gates of hell shall not prevail against it,' said Jesus.[4] We need to hold tight to this truth in a day when the mantra in our own nation seems often to be that the church is fatally haemorrhaging young people, and books like *Disappearing Church* and *Invisible Church* are being written.[5]

What are we to do? I believe we are called to believe in the church. The other side of the coin is that there are thousands of thriving churches in the UK, which are attracting hordes of young people and are places of great joy and exhilaration. Six million people regularly attend church.[6] There's more than one story about the church; we're called not to give up meeting together or encouraging one another, because church matters.[7]

That said, we must be humbly realistic about the church's failings. We need to acknowledge that people have been hurt by feeling judged or rejected by the church. We must realise that the church can be out of touch with the real questions people are asking and may have atrophied in styles of worship, communicating in ways that can no longer be heard. As Christian grandparents, we're called to talk about all these things with our grandchildren if we can, and also to invite them to 'come and see', as Philip replied to Nathanael when he asked, 'Can anything good come out of Nazareth?'[8] Today our grandchildren might well ask us, 'Can anything good come out of the church?'

I've had a few bad experiences myself, so I can identify with people's cautious approach to church. Perhaps you have too. When I was 17, having failed to gain a place at the college of my choice, I instead signed up for King Alfred's in Winchester. I'd spent the best part of the previous year as an au pair to two different families in France, discovering the delights (and dangers) of adult freedom. I had gained an appetite for discussing politics in cafes (this was 1968, when students protested en masse against capitalism and consumerism), French philosophy, North African men and fun in general. Mesmerised by the intriguing international crowd I found myself among on my 'course for foreigners', all of them much older than me, I had a hugely exciting year. So I did not arrive in Winchester ready to repent of my sins and knuckle down to serious study. Being curious by nature, I accepted an invitation to the college's Christian Union. My memory of this one-and-only visit has faded but for a couple of details: it was full of serious-looking girls with drab clothes and stern hairstyles, and there were no boys (a crucial ingredient of any group I was going to join). I have no idea what was talked about or what happened; I only knew that I never wanted to go back. This says something about who we are being more influential than what we say. As D.L. Moody said, 'Out of 100 men, one will read the Bible; the other 99 will read the Christian.'[9]

Jesus said, 'I have come that they may have life, and have it to the full.'[10] Conveying the joy of living in the presence, and with the advice, of Jesus and the joy of friendship in the Christian community will bring the light of understanding, which brings more joy. Children are inquisitive and excited, so I want to be inquisitive and excited with them, attentive to the moment.

As I write, I am looking at what for me is one of the most beautiful sights in the world – a tidal estuary on the Pembrokeshire coast. It is a landscape and seascape that is never still, but in perpetual motion, thanks to the tide, the rolling sea and the drifting, shifting clouds. Often the whole scene will suddenly light up, sharpening every line and contour, colour and shape. It's as if huge heavenly stage lights have suddenly been switched on at the director's command: 'Take 52; take a million billion!' Every time this happens, I feel my heart expand with joy. It's not that without the sun, the scene is not lovely; countless times we have remarked that no matter where you stand in this little coastal corner, the beauty is breathtaking. Even when the November tides lash the sea wall and the sky is dark and brooding, we see beauty. But there's no denying that the flash of sunlight makes you catch your breath in awe. Light brings joy, and God is the source of all beauty and joy. Every part of the natural world that humans have not disfigured in their greed and lust for wealth and power receives these bursts of light that birth joy, whether for a second or for long minutes. My beloved corner may be in Pembrokeshire, but you have yours, too.

In the same way, I have so often experienced an inner fire of joy among a worshipping community. Augustine of Hippo famously said, 'Our hearts are restless till they find their rest in thee.'[11] He believed that whatever you are enjoying, God is the source of your joy. As Michael Mayne writes:

> The thing you love is from him and is lovely because it bears his signature. All joy is really found in God, and anything you do enjoy is derivative, because what you are really looking for is him, whether you know it or not.[12]

Just as I did not find joy at that Christian Union meeting long ago, I want to make sure I don't pass on any idea that God is dull and disapproving, or is against fun and laughter, but rather that, like the light, he brings joy.

I suppose much of what this book is about is asking for the wisdom to pitch things appropriately for the age of the child. You and I change with the passing of the years, and as grandparents some of us may now enjoy reading Morning, Evening and Night Prayer from Daily Prayer.[13] But nothing could be more tedious for children! All that monotonous repetition and those long words.

I was recently invited back to my old school to preach. My memories of chapel are faint, but the clearest one is that it was boring. To this day, I can't remember a single thing I ever heard there. Perhaps I would have if the people who felt they had something to transmit and who passionately believed in what they had to say had come to preach. (But perhaps they did, and I was a path that they scattered their seed on and the birds came and ate it up, which Jesus explains as being snatched away through lack of understanding.[14]) The hymns were dreary, the liturgy painful and in those days there was no heating, which didn't help any concentration there might have been.

Today's chaplain is a delightful young ordained woman who I wish had been the chaplain when I was a girl. When I enquired about the format of the service, she said, 'We sing one song, then I'll get one of the girls to do your reading, then it's your message (15 minutes max), then I'll say a couple of prayers. We'll sing a last hymn, and that's it – half an hour tops.'

Brilliant! She's cutting her cloth to fit the garment. It was Epiphany Sunday, the first service of the year, so she was smiley, welcoming and kindly encouraging to the girl who read the lesson. Apparently, the best thing I said was that when I was at the school, I never wanted to be at chapel, and I didn't suppose they wanted to be there either! I hope that even one of them might remember in years to come my explanation of why I did want to be there now, talking about Jesus. I'm sure many of them will remember one or other of the many people who visit to give their 15 minutes, because the young chaplain there believes with all her heart that Jesus is the way, the truth and the life, and that choosing for or against him is the most important decision we will ever make or not make – and therefore she invites people who also believe this and who want to facilitate the faith of open-minded youngsters.

I didn't pitch things entirely appropriately – bathed in the amniotic fluid of the city of dreaming spires for 16 years, which churns out scholars, post-docs, researchers and genii of all disciplines, I went a bit Oxfordy on them and referenced something Kierkegaard winsomely said about Epiphany. Mea culpa. But I had them most of the time.

In thinking about church, I want to make sure my grandchildren don't think that God is only to be found on a Sunday morning in a large building where they must sit still and listen to someone saying lots of long and funny words that bear no relation to the rest of their week. Christian community is so much broader than the Sunday, so much bigger than a building. At the same time, I want to avoid giving the impression that my church gets how to do church, therefore implying that others don't. What we offer our children and youth *is* pretty good, substantial and age-appropriate. I'm proud of our children's pastor and church and, while no church has the perfect children's menu, I think we deliver a healthy, soul-building diet to all the young. But so do many others, and that's my message to my grandchildren.

Another important message for children is that it's okay to be sad. In the same way that light constantly shifts in a landscape, so joy is a moving feast in the human soul, and is sometimes more like a deep underground stream than a scintillating fountain. Children have a natural capacity for joy; pain and difficulty usually lie ahead of them. They don't live in the past or the future, as adults often do, but are attuned to the moment. However, sometimes suffering comes to a child, both through huge things, such as illness, death or parental divorce, and small things that look huge to the child, such as rejection in the playground or being taunted about their appearance.

I still remember today the experience of suddenly having to board at my school, because my mother was ill, which was traumatising. I was eight years old and had just been given an unflattering bowl cut, a strange custom of the 1950s. I made my first appearance as a boarder to jeers of 'You look like a bo-oy; you look like a bo-oy.' 'So what?' you say, 'were you a bit of a wet drip?' Maybe, but I had had no time to process the sudden change of scene from safe home to scary boarding school, and the trauma in the experience was such that I lost control of my bowels, first through severe constipation and then as a result of being forced to take a big dose of syrup of figs every evening, dispensed by fierce matron, to correct the situation.

Another issue to think about, if our grandchildren do go to church, is the biblical material they are introduced to. We need to think hard about which Bible stories we introduce children to, and at what age we do so. 'Isn't it obvious?' you ask. It isn't. There are shedloads of Sunday-school material that wades through all the Bible stories irrespective of their X-rated or otherwise unsuitable content, on the grounds that it's good for children to discover the whole Bible. Yes, it is, but not when they are four years old. My four-year-old granddaughter came home from church with her mother one Sunday with an A4 picture of Abraham, knife raised over a bound Isaac, which she, like all the other children, had been colouring in. She did not say, 'Look at my picture, Mummy,' expecting admiration of her colouring skills. She asked in a worried voice and with a frown, 'Mummy, why did Abraham want to kill his son?'

The Bible contains as much horror, violence, sex, perversion, war and misery as any other book. It is arguably more of a skill to introduce children gradually to its pages than to unveil its depths to adults, yet so often children are presented with a series of famous and colourful stories, parts of which simply do not have a U rating. Many of them don't even have a PG rating. All right, Daniel escaped being eaten alive by lions; but what about Daniel's accusers?

> At the king's command, the men who had falsely accused Daniel were brought in and thrown into the lions' den, along with their wives and children. And before they reached the floor of the den, the lions overpowered them and crushed all their bones.[15]

So many questions are raised by just this one verse – vengeance without trial; violence; punishing the innocent with the guilty; feeding animals with humans – that a depth of spiritual and theological insight and understanding beyond the comprehension of any child are obviously necessary for this to make any sense at all. We are often thoughtless in our approach to conveying God's truth to children. When talking about their experience of church, many say,

'I used to go to Sunday school, but I left after that and never went back.' I wonder if all this may be part of the underlying reason why?

When the time comes, we have to be honest about the church's history, which is littered with conflict and schism. In my own city of Oxford, bishops Thomas Cranmer, Hugh Latimer and Nicholas Ridley were burnt to death for their Protestant faith, while Oxford-educated Catholic Edmund Campion, after whom the Jesuit Campion Hall is named, was tortured and put to death in the reign of Queen Elizabeth I.

Since we nailed our colours to the flag of Christ over 40 years ago, we have almost always had Catholic friends, beginning with our French friend Genevieve. She and her husband were members of the first church we served, and it's true that we didn't really learn much about Catholicism itself, but we smelt its aroma in the bearing and being of Genevieve. Later, in France itself for ten years, we deliberately courted cross-party friendship, so to speak, and through founding a Catholic-Protestant conference, became good friends with a Jesuit. Probably my favourite speaking engagement of all was sharing a platform with our Jesuit friend Guy. Looking back, I marvel at his graciousness in agreeing to do so, not only with a woman, but with one so young and inexperienced. Today in Oxford, we are good friends with Jesuit Father Nick King. On one occasion, after lunch with him and the community, he gave us a tour of the treasure trove that is the Hall, home as it is to scores of beautiful and hugely valuable, if not invaluable, works of art – paintings, reliefs, sculptures, altar pieces, murals and furniture. One is a lithograph of the martyr Edmund Campion by Eric Gill. Beneath it is a Latin inscription commemorating his death at the hands of evil and heretical Protestants. Nick, who reads Latin fluently, read this out, pausing to apologise with a grin for the harsh judgement on our tribe – and we all laughed.

We were able to laugh because these denominational differences, most extremely exemplified in the centuries-old hostilities between

Catholicism and Protestantism, are rapidly becoming a thing of the past, as the walls come down. Now we know that Catholics and Protestants both bring insight and treasure to the table – knowledge of God and beautiful holiness in their respective saints, both past and present. We know that all denominations, old and new, communicate good things about God and his nature. We seem to have understood that no denomination gets everything right, and that no human being is without their flaws. Famously and tragically, Martin Luther, who released the Bible from its prison into the hands of the everyman, and delivered the wonderful truth that salvation is found through faith in Jesus, not through the church and its structures, was also consistently anti-Semitic.

I don't want my grandchildren ever to be given the feeling that the right thing to be is a particular brand of Protestant, or that any one person – let alone us, God forbid – really knows everything and is also right about everything they know (with the exception of Jesus Christ). My church history has taken me though 'label land'. I have been an evangelical, charismatic, Baptist (both a member of a Baptist church and baptised as an adult), and most recently have enjoyed the renaissance of interest in history's monastics and contemplatives.

I love exploring the contemplative tradition, and am drawn to what a rule of life, for example, brings into the daily round; but I don't want to be labelled a contemplative.

I am persuaded that God, who is love, longs for every human being to know themselves loved, more deeply and comprehensively than any human can love. In this sense, I love being an evangelical – I believe that, however it happens, whether through a slow process, like John Bunyan, or through blinding revelation, like D.L. Moody or Wesley, feeling his heart 'strangely warmed', discovering the reality and love of God through Jesus is the desired destiny of every human life. But I don't want to be labelled an evangelical.

I am absolutely persuaded that the gifts of the Holy Spirit, as listed in 1 Corinthians 12, Romans 12 and Ephesians 4, are for today in the same way that they were given for the early church. Prophetic words of insight, or words that contain knowledge that can only have been acquired supernaturally; healing of body, mind, soul and spirit; having faith for something that is way beyond the comprehension of most people; talking to God in a language peculiar to the individual, and other than one's mother tongue; being given the supernatural ability to understand and translate a language you have never learnt, be it angelic or human – I have seen and heard all these gifts in operation, and in general they do good. In that sense, I am a charismatic. But equally I have encountered abuses, and I don't want to be labelled a charismatic.

As for being Baptist, a lot of heat is generated among the committed about when you can or should be baptised. All I want to say about this is that, just as marriage is public, to show that we are committing our lives to each other, so it is right and proper to make our commitment to Jesus public. If Jesus himself was baptised, saying, 'It is proper for us to do this to fulfil all righteousness,'[16] that's good enough for me. After years of listening to impassioned arguments about the timing of baptism, I think there's plenty of biblical support for both infant and adult baptism, and that's what I'll be telling my grandchildren. (But that's for you to explore if it interests you.) And, correct, I don't want to be called either a Baptist or a paedo-Baptist.

If you need to label me, call me a Christian, a follower of Jesus Christ. I aspire to my grandchildren showing equal respect and attention to anyone who is a follower of Christ, whatever their shade and style.

Children's impressions of church are shaped and dictated by so many things: whether they grow up in a churchgoing family, and if they do whether they actually enjoy their experience of church; the attitude of their parents to faith and religion in general, churchgoing or not; school and friends; film and TV – it's sad, but not surprising, that the majority of movies and TV programmes that deal with faith and religion do so in a negative or mocking way. Conscious of all these influences, I pray that I may speak well and respectfully, but also truthfully and honestly, of the church with my grandchildren.

'Christian' is a word that embraces a vast spectrum of convictions and beliefs. Like everyone else, I situate myself at a certain spot on the continuum – in fact, more like the variation in bandwidth of a radio station than a spot. It's unlikely that my grandchildren will pick up the soundwaves at exactly the same place, but I hope and pray that gentle and respectful conversations will take place as they grow up and into their adulthood, and that in time they will come to love the church in all its finery and failings, its mistakes and mystery, its resistance and radiance.

The German martyr Dietrich Bonhoeffer deeply understood the paradoxical nature of church:

> The more genuine and the deeper our community becomes, the more will everything else between us recede, the more clearly and purely will Jesus Christ and his work become the one and only thing that is vital between us. We have one another only through Christ, but through Christ we do have one another, wholly, and for all eternity.[17]

This speaks of a committed and compassionate community, the kind of community I love and believe I belong to as I write, and the kind of community I pray my grandchildren might find.

9

Shifting tectonic plates: culture's changing landscape

The primary effects of earthquakes are ground shaking, ground rupture, landslides and tsunamis. Fires are probably the most important secondary effect of earthquakes.

Greg Anderson[1]

Jesus Christ is the same yesterday and today and for ever.

HEBREWS 13:8

As a child in the 1950s I grew up in a reserved culture where things like politics, religion and sex were never discussed. With regard to politics, it was not until I spent some months in France in 1968 that I encountered the exhilarating world of political discussion, always in cafes and accompanied by *grands crèmes*, wine or Pernod (depending on the time of day) and wreathed in smoke from Gauloises cigarettes. With regard to religion, although a churchgoer throughout my childhood, faith was assumed rather than discussed or explained. With regard to sex, as a teenager in the 1960s, I would blush to utter – or even think of – words to do with sex and sexuality; they were still confined to top-shelf magazines, often wrapped in brown paper.

Nearly five decades on, the language of politics, religion and sexuality is not only everyday currency, but frequently to be read right across the media, from tabloids to highbrow publications. There remains a tiny vestige of restraint when it comes to broadcasting, but it probably won't be long before the final fence falls and this language will be added to the vocabulary of the national newscasters, as it has already been to that of the arts and literary worlds.

Before we examine how this has happened and whether it is all bad, the point of this chapter is to paint a picture of the cultural background against which we aspire to be loving and supportive grandparents, and to remind us of what a very different world we inhabit from that of our own grandparents. In the apostle Peter's first letter to the early church, he writes, 'Be ready to speak up and tell anyone who asks why you're living the way you are, and always with the utmost courtesy.'[2]

It's important to say right away that nostalgia for the 'good old days' is misplaced. Many things about the 21st century are an improvement on the previous one, all the way from health and longevity to our understanding of the human psyche. We might say, for example, that the restraint of the 20th-century world hid a great hypocrisy, while today there is much greater freedom of expression, openness and honesty about anything and everything; no longer are there things that are off limits for public discussion.

But it's easy to throw out the baby with the bathwater, and arguably the absence of discretion in the name of free speech that we witness today can lead to unbridled licence, which in turn can lead to tragic consequences as well as more so-called freedom.

How has this happened, then? Halfway through the 20th century, Britain could still be described as Christian. Church still played a role in the lives of most people. For many, that role may have been superficial, but church provided an anchor and represented some sort of order. Then came the swinging '60s, which saw the casting off of restraint, a bad thing, as old taboos were broken, often a good thing.

Throughout the latter decades of the century, as improvements in modes of travel and the birth of the European Union made migration easier, we gradually became a multicultural and increasingly secular society, with the inevitable consequence that the influence of Christianity steadily waned. The old givens of faith are, therefore, no longer here. The church overall continues to haemorrhage young people, and this means we can't assume that our grandchildren will share our beliefs about God in the way that our grandparents could assume that of us.

While massive cultural changes were taking place like great subterranean earthquakes, everything to do with sexuality and gender was beginning to shift. The women's liberation movement brought emancipation for women in every area of life, and the development of the internet and social media began to change the way in which and the speed at which people conducted relationships. Among the beliefs and convictions that have most radically evolved in the last 70 years are those around sexual ethics. The noughties brought an explosion of online pornography, and as sexual caution was thrown to the winds, our culture became increasingly sexualised in all sorts of ways, from the world of advertising, to the language of the media, to the ugly phenomenon of date rape and the profile of sexual crime. More recently, in 2017, as pain and anger against sexual aggression rightly boiled over, the seminal #MeToo movement was born, then baptised by Oprah Winfrey at the 2018 Golden Globes Ceremony.

There is an irony about #MeToo in that it was birthed out of an entertainment culture that often seems to promote (predominantly male) promiscuity. Finding appropriate boundaries in a climate where sexual freedom is advocated is a huge challenge for the young – and indeed for everyone. An example of the power of this dark culture is the advent of online agencies making it easy for married people to have an affair; one such service even advertised on motorway billboards with the slogan 'The grass is always greener'. That, however, is dwarfed by the porn industry, reputed to be the world's largest money-making enterprise.

It's not that human sexual behaviour has changed; what has changed is how explicit it now is. Many good things have resulted from these societal changes, an outstanding example being the decriminalisation of homosexuality in 1967; but we are also living with less good consequences of the outing of all things sexual, too.

One of these is our present confusion about sexual ethics, and some dis-ease between men and women about how to relate to each other. Some men have retreated into passivity; others are unsure how to strike the right note with women. We see what can seem like stridency in some women, but really this is an expression of self-protection and a reaction to great injustices in the past. For both men and women, these things can lead to the danger of suppressed anger, born of pain and frustration, which can risk erupting into public conflict, or worse, into violence.

Is this climate of outspokenness all bad? Definitely not. In fact, for us as grandparents today we have an advantage that our own grandparents never had. We can probably talk to our grandchildren much more openly, without shame or embarrassment, in a way that would never have been possible for us with our grandparents. In fact, if it is true that breaking through taboos leads to unfettered discussion about anything, then it could lead to discussions about God and faith, and maybe even about sex. Of course, we aspire to talk with our grandchildren about all sorts of other things, too, in an age-appropriate way – poverty, the environment, justice, war and politics. A teenager may or may not become fascinated and passionate about any one of these, but they are very likely to become fascinated by sex at some point.

Sex may or may not become a subject of conversation, but if it did, what kind of things might we say? Most Christians have convictions about sex and sexuality that they try to live by. But if this is true of you and me, we must remember that we can't assume our grandchildren will share our convictions. So why have we chosen to live as we do with regard to marriage and sex? One day we may find the conversation turns to this subject. If so, it will help to know why we have the convictions we do; we don't want to become flustered or defensive because we can't explain why.

Let's look first at the Bible's expression of perfect equality between the sexes, right from the start:

> So God created mankind in his own image, in the image of God he created them; male and female he created them.[3]

It's interesting that no other ancient creation narrative talks about special creation of woman – it is only the biblical creation account that highlights its importance, emphasising God's intended equality between the sexes. In Genesis 3, we read how this beautiful equality was disfigured at the fall, leading to centuries of disorder and division between the sexes, until Jesus re-establishes the original equality through all his interactions with both women and men.

There are lots of examples in the gospels of Jesus breaking through the inequalities of social and religious traditions and convention, perhaps most famously in his encounter with the Samaritan woman at the well, described in John 4. Not only did Jews historically discriminate against the Samaritans, treating them as a despised and powerless minority, but the religious did not mix with 'sinners' and, most importantly here, men did not speak with women. Jesus' prolonged conversation with a woman in public flew in the face of the conventions of the time.

As John Stott wrote, 'Without any fuss or publicity Jesus terminated the curse of the fall, reinvested woman with her partially lost nobility and reclaimed for his new kingdom community the original creation blessing of sexual equality.'[4]

Jesus broke down the barriers and divisions between men and women at every turn, yet today it seems that the sexes are still at war. How did we get here? If I had to give a simple answer it would be that the tension between the ways of God and the ways of human beings, and between men and women, is reflected throughout history, and the gradual emergence of humanism as a prevailing philosophy has ensured its survival. In Ecclesiastes we read that God has 'set eternity in the human heart',[5] which means that we are designed to worship. We can't help worshipping just as we can't help breathing; if we don't worship God, we will worship something or someone else. Youth, beauty and money are some of the gods of today, but the worship of these things depletes rather than energises us.

We are living in a day of undeniable tension between the sexes, though thankfully rigorous and thorough safeguarding policies aimed at protection for all are coming into place, particularly in the work arena. Despite this, there is a sense of persistent inequality between the sexes that seems impossible to root out of our culture. One example of this is the issue of equal pay. The popular Netflix series *The Crown* was criticised for awarding higher pay to Matt Smith, who plays Prince Philip, than to Claire Foy, who plays Elizabeth II, a far more substantial role. At the same time, a great furore broke out about unequal pay for male and female broadcasters, and Sarah Montague made a much-publicised move from BBC Radio 4's morning news programme, *Today*, to its lunchtime programme, *The World at One*, to restore equilibrium. An easier example for most of us to relate to is found in the home. Although progress has been made, for example in the granting of paternity leave following the birth of a child, it is still true that where both parents are employed, the lion's share of domestic maintenance tends to be carried by the woman.

The internet provides plenty of information about the changing world of sexual identity. For example:

> The term LGBTQIAPD is an extended version of LGBT. The difference between the two is that the former takes into account a wider range of sexualities and gender identities. It stands for Lesbian, Gay, Bisexual, Transgender, Queer/Questioning, Intersexual, Asexual, Pansexual/Polysexual and Demisexual.[6]

Having the information is one thing; understanding it is quite another, both for a child and also for a grandparent. This is likely to be new territory for many of us. As a young adult, the only transgender person I met was the author Jan Morris, previously James Morris, with whose son I was at university. At the time Jan had a high profile, but I think she provoked more of a curious than a campaigning spirit, not least because she was pretty much alone out there at the time.

How are we to understand these bewildering changes? In my view one key is found in the book of Genesis. The story of the fall, which follows hard on the heels of the beautiful creation account, helps us understand the culture in which we find ourselves as grandparents today, with God pushed to the far margins, if visible at all.

All through history, rejection of the one in whose care Christians believe humanity can be safe has ebbed and flowed. Today in the west, the flow of rejection is strong, despite the growing evidence of spiritual hunger expressed in all kinds of spiritual activities and practices. The beautiful balance of relationship between Adam and Eve, and the trust between them, is lost through their competition with God, and it brings pain for both, in the labour of work and the labour of childbirth. This distortion from the original plan – 'God saw all that he had made, and it was very good'[7] – has continued in different ways in different cultures all down the centuries and is still present today.

The Bible tells us a lot about sexual equality. What does it say about family? It would be hard to deny that the fundamental pattern demonstrated throughout the Bible is that of mother, father and children, and, in fact, grandchildren, since family in the Hebrew culture included extended family, which is still far more common across many different cultures than the chiefly western form of the nuclear family. This is not to say that the families depicted across the pages of the Bible were all good, holy and happy. Far from it.

In their book *Keeping Faith*, Jo Swinney and Katharine Hill write:

> What we believe inevitably works its way out in how we behave, and if our children (or grandchildren) do not share our Christian convictions, the chances that they are going to sign up to a Christian code of behaviour are slim to none. This is not to say that Christians have a monopoly on good character or standards of morality or a sense of social responsibility – we all know that isn't the case.

They go on to say that, since the Christian way is not the norm,

> we can be in danger of getting sexual sin out of all proportion. We could be so blinded by the enormity of the sexual stuff going on where it shouldn't be that we miss all the good things going on: the stirrings of compassion for the poor or righteous anger at injustice; a spiritual hunger that's leading them to pray even as they are unsure whom they are addressing; a sense that they can't shake off that they are part of a bigger story…

> I don't mean to imply that how we behave sexually is irrelevant. It matters to us, and it matters to God. But bring to mind the sexual record of some of the biblical characters beloved of God and you have to admit it doesn't seem to be a deal-breaker. Abraham slept with his wife's servant – at his wife's suggestion; David committed adultery; Solomon had 700 wives and 300 concubines.[8]

We could make this list a lot longer: Judah fathered a baby by his daughter-in-law (and was under the impression he was sleeping with a prostitute when the child was conceived) and David's son Amnon raped his half-sister Tamar, his spent lust turning immediately to hatred and leading to extreme family chaos. All these things are still experienced in families today, including families whose members are Christians, with terrible, ongoing and sometimes tragic consequences.

Today's family models are hugely varied: two-parent families, whether two mothers, two fathers or one of each; single-parent families; blended families; extended families; parents who are married, cohabiting and divorced.

Any of us could find ourselves becoming a part of any of these models of family, and for many of us as Christians this can bring both challenge and heartache. But if we are mindful of the colourful and chaotic panoply of family spread across the pages of the Bible, it will remind us that we are called to behave within and towards our families – particularly, for the purposes of this book, our grandchildren – as God always has towards his people throughout the ages (including ourselves): with unfailing love, mercy, grace and kindness.

The grace God offers can't be withdrawn on the day a young person, for example, declares themself gay. But we should remember that despite the wide and rightful acceptance of the LGBTQI community, welcoming it personally still demands great courage for some.

Many Christians may have experienced heartache and angst over the redefinition of marriage passed in the Marriage (Same Sex Couples) Act of 2013 in the UK. We may have deep and strong convictions about marriage, rooted in our understanding of the Bible. We may even feel that the new marriage law is completely at odds with the very meaning of marriage. All of this considered – including our own history and experience – we must constantly ask ourselves, 'What's dictating my approach to my grandchildren? Is it my beliefs and convictions, or is it the unconditional love of Christ?'

Modern blended families, as families with step-parents are often called, come with their own challenges, usually felt mostly in adapting to the 'new' parent or being accepted by the 'new' child. The global village we all inhabit adds a further dimension to the dynamics. James' wife died of cancer several years ago, and he is now with a new girlfriend, Patricia, whose husband died unexpectedly of a heart attack. James says, 'My daughter Annabel is ambivalent towards Patricia; she is still feeling acutely the loss of her mother, specially now she has her own child Sammy, so with her parents-in-law in South Africa, she feels the absence of a grandmother acutely.'

On the agony uncles' and aunts' pages of the papers we can find pain-filled letters about this from people who wouldn't call themselves Christians, and so are without the comfort that this can bring in such circumstances. I came across one such letter written to an agony uncle, from a woman on her 70th birthday. Far from being happy, because everyone says she looks young for her age and her husband spoils her, she is miserable because none of her three stepchildren have ever sent her a card or given her a present, despite seeing her every week. She and her husband both have children and grandchildren, but it seems that her stepdaughter is not happy about her grandchildren's close relationship with her husband. So her dream of both sets of grandchildren coming to play together at her home remains a dream.

The reply contains some good advice: 'Why didn't your husband have the gumption to remind his children to send you a card and flowers? Divorces aren't easy for anyone, but while a second marriage can soothe your pain it often makes things even worse for the children... people have been hurt along the way, and they will never play happy families just to please you... This isn't what you imagined being a grandparent would be like, but this is the way things have turned out. It's not long trestle tables groaning with food, and laughing adults passing the wine while small children run around a sun-soaked lawn.' So far, so humorous, and certainly wise in its realism, but it ends with a rather curt instruction to 'lower your expectations'.[9]

Lowering our expectations is generally a good thing to do, but there's no advice or encouragement here to try to communicate about these things, which is surprising in a culture where we are often encouraged to reach out. And inevitably, there is no hint of the sort of advice we might glean from the Bible's counsel about the possible mending of what is broken. Little comfort is really offered to a woman who is expressing pain.

An agony aunt may be a skilled counsellor. More importantly, however, am I a good person to give advice to a grandchild? All I may offer without it being asked for is love and kindness. I may offer advice, but only if I am asked for it; and if I ever were asked for such advice maybe I have more in my bag of tools than most agony columnists, because my whole being is soaked in a decades-long walk with Jesus. This is not about the wonderful and wise person I am, but about the majestic character of Jesus Christ, who bestrides time and space and humanity; it is about my grasp, however slender, of 'how wide and long and high and deep is the love of Christ', and my years of leaning in to 'know this love that surpasses knowledge'.[10]

I'm not for one moment suggesting that to be a good counsellor you have to be a Christian; counselling is a complex art, and Christians can be terrible at it. Psychotherapy, psychology and medical science have made vast strides in understanding the human psyche over the course of the same decades that have seen the near disappearance of God from our culture, and many secular counsellors are outstanding in their discipline. And there are, of course, some excellent agony aunts and uncles.

To put the finishing touches to this rough sketch of the cultural canvas of the past 70 years, the picture is far from all bad. Since the terrible revelations of how Jimmy Savile fixed a lot of other things besides the dreams of children – mostly the well-being of dozens of young girls and women into a coffin of trauma and mental ill-health (until or unless raised to life) – the domino effect has continued, peaking and troughing, but ploughing steadily onwards, as emboldened by one another, woman after woman has opened up about her experience of harassment or abuse.

While we must celebrate the fact that behaviour shockingly tolerated during the 1970s and 1980s will no longer be so, there are downsides to the tsunami of revelations and the resulting bans and exclusions. The most important of these is that the power of social media to whip up crowd responses has led in some quarters to extremes of reaction. In our desire to be politically correct and ruthless towards impropriety, vindictiveness can replace justice.

The nervousness that stalks relations between men and women means that it's increasingly difficult to be free in our affections, and if we are by nature tactile we must be very circumspect. Trust between men and women is fragile, reflecting the estrangement that first came between them so long ago in the garden of Eden.

Sometimes a story of conflict that has resulted in injury or worse hits the headlines, but it provokes uncertainty as well as outrage and disgust. We may find ourselves wondering who's telling the truth, and it may be that the truth will never be known; uncertainty may linger in our minds and in the media. The cultural landscape we are walking in is ever more complex, making the pursuit of true justice seem like panning for gold.

Where have grandparents come to in this? Maybe to a better understanding of how complex it is to think and feel and talk about these things. Maybe to a stronger conviction of the need for equality and justice between the sexes. Maybe to a better grasp of a strange new sexual landscape that includes a vast number of gender identities available to choose from (the social networking website Tumblr lists 112). And then maybe to the realisation that we are all searching for a language that can unite rather than divide, that can speak peace.

This, in turn, could mean that we grandparents might be good people for our grandchildren to talk to when they are confused or frightened, or during the storms of adolescence, as they try to work out who they are in a Babel-like world of confusing language.

Let's choose to be such people, unshockable and unafraid of the multifarious social and sexual landscape we all now inhabit and that will help us, whatever our grandchildren's life choices, to offer one of the most precious gifts a grandparent can give – unconditional love.

10

Keeping faith when faith is in question

I have no notion of loving people by halves; it is not my nature.
Jane Austen[1]

We live by faith, not by sight.
2 CORINTHIANS 5:7

The word that keeps coming to mind is 'safe'. I want us as grandparents to be safe people and a safe place for our grandchildren. Safe as a place of shelter, where the pressures of the world don't intrude and the giants and monsters can't reach them. But also safe in terms of their certainty that they will always be welcome, always find encouragement, and never any censorship about a life choice, a point of view or a decision.
Juliet

Our high calling is to avoid ever giving any grandchild – child, teenager or adult – the feeling that we reject them because of what they think or do; it is to love them unreservedly and to make this known by our kindness, generosity and words. If we find, as we almost certainly will, that we radically disagree with someone, we have to make sure that this doesn't communicate (or indeed reflect) disapproval or rejection of them as a person. We may be unable to condone a choice or decision, but we must choose to love unconditionally – to separate our feelings about the actions or opinions of someone we love from our unassailable love for them. This is much more challenging today, on the back of the societal sea changes I've alluded to, than it was a couple of generations ago.

I absolutely share Juliet's expression of undying love and the desire to be a safe haven for her grandchildren. Yes, I will love them forever, no matter what they do or become. Nothing they say or do will ever cause me to withdraw from them or initiate any kind of estrangement. This is a daring declaration, but I want to throw down the gauntlet.

Many of us have probably struggled to come to terms with the evolution of culture since our childhood, and the progressive enshrinement of the changes in law to accommodate it. There's a lot of noise around issues that touch us personally – the beginning and end of life, sexual identity, freedom of expression and the right not to be offended. I believe this noise conceals something more profound, namely the creeping suppression of our freedom of conscience. The other day I read an article entitled 'The dictatorship of diversity'. Of course diversity is essential, but not as a dictator.

Part of the reason for writing this book is to fly the flag for freedom of conscience. Love is king, but you and I, and every human being, must be free thinkers, bearing as we do the image of God – the *imago dei*. Whatever we may think (and we should have the freedom of conscience to think as we like), what's at stake here is our freedom to agree to disagree agreeably.

When deeply held and felt views are challenged, it can trigger an emotive eruption. Who has not experienced this at some moment in their lives over some issue? Even relatively impersonal matters, such as the legalisation of cannabis or some other political decision, can generate great heat. A family whose members all identify as Christian will still reflect a wide diversity of opinion, so if we disagree we must do so peaceably.

For our grandchildren, by far the most important thing is their unshakeable assurance that we view them with 'unconditional positive regard'.[2]

The march and conquest of what we term political correctness has sometimes resulted in the expression either of a different point of view or of a strong conviction being classed as a criminal offence, and Christians have sometimes found themselves unexpectedly catapulted into the legal arena. My own experience here is of being summoned to a tribunal, along with five others, for a religious offence. While serving on the board of a Christian academic institution, I had prayed for a Jewish colleague, with her permission, and our conversations had included the topic of church; but because relations with other colleagues deteriorated over a period of time, I and five faculty and staff members eventually found ourselves in court. Although we won the case, it was a sobering experience and a reminder of the care we need to take over our words and actions.

Because of a failure to agree to disagree agreeably, the world is full of families with estranged members. This is often due to a row or longstanding disagreement, but sometimes it's because of life choices. As grandparents let's hope and pray we may communicate our covenant love for each grandchild at an appropriate, God-given time, but until – and beyond – that time, we're called to live it as well as declare it.

'I may not always agree with your choices in life, but I will love you forever.' How do we navigate disagreement and divergence of opinion in a way that doesn't sully a relationship? How do we remain true to our conscience and convictions while at the same time avoiding coming over as judgemental or critical? Let's be clear that being with someone, sharing time and activities with them, whether watching a movie or going on holiday, is not the same as agreeing with or condoning the choices they have made. So often we are confused about this.

I have never forgotten Dianne Parsons, of Care for the Family, sharing an anecdote from when her son was a teenager. Dianne had been seen out shopping with her son's girlfriend and was greeted at church the following Sunday by a starchy-faced person, who asked, 'How can you condone your son going out with a non-Christian?' (The question itself is a problem.) Dianne wisely and wittily replied, 'I wasn't condoning it; I was shopping with her.'

So what do we *do* when it comes to actually letting them know that we believe in Jesus and have chosen to be his follower? How do we live our love for these children? There are things we can do when they are with us, and things we can say in conversations.

For some fortunate grandparents, babysitting the grandchildren so that their parents can go out or even go to work is a practical form of love. If this is you, you'll probably be able to go to school plays, concerts and sports days, which helps you keep in touch with what they are doing and feeling, and also what each child enjoys and is good at, as well as what they don't like.

For many grandparents, though, this familiarity is harder won. For those of us who don't live close by, technology affords us easy access through any form of social media that we have the courage to engage with. For younger children, the dying art of writing postcards and letters needs to be revived. Again, the initiative needs to be ours for as long as it takes to build sufficient relationship for a child to be motivated to communicate. Then, when they come to visit you, be ready to teach and involve them in anything that interests them, be it cooking or carpentry, music or movies. And learn from them.

Juliet says:

> If there is ever a one-to-one conversation about what I believe… I always say that in the end the most important thing is that they know that Jesus *loves* them. This is *far* more important than them thinking that they must love Jesus… I also

encourage them all the time to use their brains… especially the teenagers… and question, question, question. If there is a God and he is who he says he is, he can withstand every question and every doubt being thrown at him. We must respect the intelligence of each child… There is nothing more off-putting for a modern-day teenager than to be told what to believe… But I challenge them all the time about why they have made up their minds in a certain direction… because I want them to look at every possibility. In conversations about other religions, other races, other sexual orientations, I remind them that God has created each and every human being on the planet, and we must respect the other, and always try to imagine what it must be like to stand in another person's shoes.

Richard says:

Be willing to discuss anything with them: religion, politics, death, marriage, sex. I had a wonderful conversation with a grandson when his hormones kicked in, and his comment was, 'Thank goodness someone in the family understands teenagers!' Let them know what your values are, but make sure you listen to their views, which will be interesting. Love them because you love them, not for what they do but for who they are. Tell them where the love comes from, but not too often. Build a relationship – ultimately a trusting friendship. Remember their world is not your world of 50 or so years ago. Be willing to give them high priority in your life.

If we aspire to a trusting friendship, we must earn our grandchildren's trust. Richard continues:

Be willing to read the books they are reading, rather than trying to get them to read what you are reading. And be willing to be confidential; that is, anything they share with you remains with you and your prayers and is not passed on to other members of the family, especially their parents.

So far we have not encountered anything too tough to digest. But there are many different ways in which faith can be in question because of different life choices. In 2015, the Barna Group conducted detailed research on behalf of Care for the Family, the Church of England and the Evangelical Alliance. One key finding from this was that '42% of practising Christians attribute their faith to growing up in a Christian home. And yet it's estimated that only 50% of the children of Christian parents grow up with a personal faith of their own.'[3]

One of the subtle changes taking place in our time is the gradual shift of responsibility for a child's welfare from the parents to the state. The Convention on the Rights of the Child was designed in good faith to protect and promote the welfare of the child, and clearly it affords protection in cases where a child is abused or hurt. But making fair and just decisions is a complex business, as in the case of baby Alfie Evans, whose life support was withdrawn by the medical team in opposition to his parents' wishes.[4]

This gradual shift towards the state has a subliminal effect on parents, who can feel that school – and, in the case of Christians, also the church – bears significant responsibility for their child. Yet the Barna research discovered that a major factor in a child developing their own faith is the positive nurturing of faith by the parents; in other words, the greatest influence, for good or ill, on the faith of a child is the home. If children feel close to their parents, grow up in a warm family and see their parents developing an authentic (not perfect) faith themselves, and if they receive positive multigenerational input from the wider family and church, they are more likely to follow their parents' faith.

At the same time, the research revealed a lack of confidence on the part of many parents about effectively fulfilling this role. Juliet says:

> We always say grace. Sometimes it's formal and taken from the liturgy and sometimes it's freer and we pray for someone or

something. It is *never* long! Secondly, we go to church, even if they don't, unless they're on their own with us and too young to be left at home; in this case, we never pressure them to join in with anything, or go to the children's church. They'll feel safer with us, and safety is primordial.

This is modelling without manipulation. There are all sorts of reasons why a grandparent might face the challenge of modelling a Christian perspective in a family context where faith is not a high priority. Sometimes it's a heartbreaking challenge, stretching us to the limits of our emotional strength. Karen, alone as a Christian in her family, writes:

Trying to maintain faith that God will intervene does push me to breaking point sometimes, and exposes my inner turmoil... At times my faith seems powerless and the approach of love, gentleness and being helpful wears thin. Occasionally I feel I'm crumbling under the weight of opposition; my belief drains away and hopelessness leaks into a well of bitterness and resentment deep within me, as I feel the pain of rejection... Then I challenge myself, determining to forgive, and asking God for the fruits of the Spirit to get myself back on track. This cycle of love and pain goes on in my inner world, so hopefully they rarely notice my turmoil... but it's exhausting...

It's challenging to find the right words to water down my faith when the grandchildren ask questions about relatives dying, or heaven, or getting old. I long to be able to reassure them that God loves them and will always be there for them whatever happens.

Faith may always have been absent, as in Karen's family, or it may have been lost or diminished. There are many reasons for this. It may be because a person's needs were not met by the church; or they find church strange, hypocritical, out of touch on ethical questions or current norms of sexuality, judgemental or irrelevant;

or they think the church of today is not what Jesus had in mind and is a far cry from the early church described by the New Testament. For some, it becomes impossible to reconcile a loving God with the overwhelming injustice and suffering experienced by humanity, the cruelty of which human beings are capable or the vast dimensions of natural disasters. For others, the very concept of God appears outmoded and no longer appropriate in an age that is declared 'post-truth' – and scholarly works are charting the journey of the west to post-Christendom. A further issue is the uniqueness of Jesus, because of its implicit value judgement on other religions. And then, of course, there is the Bible.

Usually a composite of several of these – and there is much overlap – will be behind a loss of faith. It won't escape your notice that many of these contributing factors revolve around the shortcomings of the church. And nine times out of ten leaving church doesn't mean leaving God. This should give us lots of food for thought as grandparents, but also as individuals, about what sort of changes could create a more accessible church. Let's not see ourselves as not responsible for such things; rather let's believe that God grants wisdom to the elderly.[5]

In each case where a child's path has diverged from that of their parents, we have an opportunity to model ourselves on Jesus, the most radically inclusive person ever to walk the earth. Think of the story of Philip and the Ethiopian.[6] A sermon on this passage said:

> We know [the Ethiopian] is at least a God-fearer, a Gentile who adheres to the Jewish monotheism and piety. He is a eunuch, probably literally, we don't know for certain, but because of his sexual difference he will have been excluded from the temple and from Jewish worship in spite of his piety. So here we have a man who is different because of his skin colour and because he is of a sexual minority, and Philip finds himself welcoming him into the Christian faith. The fact that this convert to Christianity is from a sexual minority and a different race, ethnicity and

nationality surely calls Christians to be radically inclusive and welcoming. Philip was radically inclusive and welcoming because he was connected to Jesus and could therefore be a conduit to pass on grace and mercy and acceptance to others.[7]

One more thing following this story from the early church: I want to humbly offer some hope to anyone who may be reading this from within a much more difficult context – for example, in which the parents, your children, are in a same-sex marriage or partnership, or in which one of them is transitioning from one gender to the other. The children of such couples, whether adopted or born by surrogacy, will almost certainly have additional things to talk about if we create a place of safety and trust. We, the grandparents, will have begun the often-painful journey of adapting to a new reality long before the children arrived. We can hope that, whether or not our conviction has changed (and many people's do), we are able to offer absolutely the same enthusiasm and love for this family's life as for any other more conventional family that may be part of our nearest and dearest.

It's worth digging a little deeper here and admitting that it's almost inevitable that it's harder to achieve these ideals if our convictions remain in tension with the reality of a chosen lifestyle within our family. We'll explore practical ways of helping us to stay completely loving and affirming while remaining faithful to our own conscience in such a situation in chapter 12, but in terms of our approach being 100% loving and accepting, the challenge to us is that there should be no difference between this and any other model of family.

> You then, why do you judge your brother or sister? Or why do you treat them with contempt? For we will all stand before God's judgment seat... Each of us will give an account of ourselves to God. Therefore let us stop passing judgment on one another. Instead, make up your mind not to put any stumbling-block or obstacle in the way of a brother or sister.[8]

Accept one another, then, just as Christ accepted you, in order to bring praise to God.[9]

Be completely humble and gentle; be patient, bearing with one another in love.[10]

Let's have a look at some ways of making these words real in our lives. We all need help to live out such scriptures, whatever our circumstances.

11

A grandparent's prayers

Prayer is the easiest and hardest of all things; the simplest and the sublimest; the weakest and the most powerful; its results lie outside the range of human possibilities – they are limited only by the omnipotence of God.

E.M. Bounds[1]

Pray continually; give thanks in all circumstances.

1 THESSALONIANS 5:17–18

I wonder if you are as grateful as I am for words of the apostle Paul in Romans 8:

The Spirit helps us in our weakness. We do not know what we ought to pray for, but the Spirit himself intercedes for us through wordless groans. And he who searches our hearts knows the mind of the Spirit, because the Spirit intercedes for God's people in accordance with the will of God.[2]

The Message translation puts the first half of that passage like this:

The moment we get tired in the waiting, God's spirit is right alongside helping us along. If we don't know how or what to pray, it doesn't matter. He does our praying in and for us, making prayer out of our wordless sighs, our aching groans.[3]

One thing we certainly need to help us is prayer. While writing this book, I was privileged to spend two separate weeks in a friend's seafront cottage. Each day I would wrap myself up against the wild wind and set off along the mile-long beach to pour my heart out to the Lord as well as take some exercise. Sometimes my heart was singing as great streams of fairly coherent gratitude poured out of me; but sometimes, had you been with me, you would have struggled to understand the general direction of prayer. A lot of it was a sense of physical pressure in my chest, and there were occasional names, repeated over and over, and repeated pleadings – often for my grandchildren to find protection from harm, and often, too, for the children of friends. Nothing sophisticated or eloquent – in fact, quite the reverse – and lots of tears. Whichever it was, I knew that God was listening. Psalm 139 tells us:

> You perceive my thoughts from afar. You discern my going out and my lying down; you are familiar with all my ways. Before a word is on my tongue you, Lord, know it completely.[4]

I knew that God understood where I was coming from, and that his knowledge of me is intimate. David begins the same psalm by declaring this truth: 'You have searched me, Lord, and you know me.'[5]

We all pray for people beyond the bounds of our families as well as within them, but the greater the emotional attachment in a relationship, the greater the struggle to remain impartial and composed. Much of this book is devoted to seeking to offer hope and help to grandparents facing all manner of family situations. Most of us will feel emotionally undone from time to time, and sometimes for long seasons, because of our families. At such times, composing articulate prayers is very low on the priority list. Juliet says:

> I so want them to grow up well rounded and living life to the full with emotional intelligence. Above all, I long for them to be kind people who respect others and have their values grounded in Christian values.

As we've thought about many different aspects of what it means to be a grandparent and what is called for from us, it's obvious by now that expressing our views, let alone imposing them, is not top of the list. It's also obvious that keeping quiet can be costly, especially if we feel strongly about a course of action or what looks to us like a loss or lack of direction. I don't for one minute picture a generation of saintly grandparents exhibiting marvellous restraint at all times. Most of us will have let slip a 'Don't you think it might be better to…?' kind of sentence more than once, and then wished we'd kept our mouths shut. Jeremiah expresses the tension caused by self-restraint:

> The word of the Lord has brought me insult and reproach all day long. But if I say, 'I will not mention his word, or speak any more in his name,' his word is in my heart like a fire, a fire shut up in my bones. I am weary of holding it in; indeed I cannot.[6]

Earlier he laments:

> To whom can I speak and give warning? Who will listen to me? Their ears are closed so that they cannot hear. The word of the Lord is offensive to them; they find no pleasure in it.[7]

Separated by thousands of years from this Old Testament prophet, we can nonetheless identify with his passion and pain, especially if we are among those whose family situations are not straightforward. What's harder to identify with, and indeed questionable for us, is his calling to press through the rejection (which he did) and take the consequences, for we are not Old Testament prophets! The calling for us is to think about how best to be a blessing and support to our families, whatever their views on the word of the Lord. Our calling is to pray for them. It's imperative that we don't come across with a subliminal 'we know best' message. Our goal is to bless and encourage, not to be a reproof.

We're faced with two questions: how can we pray *for* our grandchildren? And how can we pray *with* them?

Praying *for* them

We can be sure that at least some of the Bible's grandparents prayed for their grandchildren, and not just those whose descendants were godly men and women. Surely Naomi prayed for Obed; surely Hannah prayed for the sons of Samuel who 'did not follow his ways [but] turned aside after dishonest gain and accepted bribes and perverted justice'.[8] The Bible doesn't relate how God answered her prayers, so let's not be dejected by this, but rather motivated to 'pray continually'.[9] And surely one of the reasons for Timothy's faith was the prayers of his grandmother Lois, the person in the family in whom the 'sincere faith… first lived'.[10]

Encouraged by these examples, let's think first about praying *for* our grandchildren. Clearly how we pray for them will depend on many things, especially on the stance of their parents towards faith in Jesus. But whatever this is, we are sure to pray for our children as well as our grandchildren. Each of us will pray according to the family's needs. Is a parent applying for a new job? Is the family moving house? Is a child unhappy at school? Are there health issues? Are there financial burdens and anxieties? We can let our families know that we're praying about any of these needs, and parents are generally grateful and comforted to know that they and their children are being prayed for. When it comes to more difficult issues, such as a struggling marriage, church attendance and questions of faith, our prayers really need to be kept to ourselves.

A big issue that demands our prayers is the digital world we all inhabit. It is worth here quoting a substantial section of Katharine Hill's book *Left to Their Own Devices*:

> Smartphones and online devices are good in that we use them to keep connected with our family, we have access to information at the touch of a screen and there are games and resources which are great for children – but there are also massive dangers. Even if our children don't have a smartphone,

their friends will. Young people are facing problems with pornography, internet addiction, sexting, grooming, cyberbullying and the struggle to find their worth and identity on social media. As parents, our job is to teach them how to be safe in a digital world, just as we teach them how to be safe when crossing the road.

Before parents can help their offspring navigate the digital age effectively, they need to recognise the difference in how adults and children approach digital technology.

By and large, most parents are digital visitors. They visit the internet to do a task, such as online shopping or sending an email. Once the task is done, they log off. But the younger generation are more likely to be digital residents. They have grown up with digital technology and 24/7 access to the internet, so their whole life becomes caught up in it. It's possible to be a digital resident safely, but the worry for parents occurs when they fall behind their children and fail to keep up with their digital knowledge.

When it comes to problems such a sexting, porn and internet addiction, there are two main reasons why some young people end up making unwise choices.

Scientists have discovered that, in a teenager's brain, the prefrontal cortex is still developing – and that's the part that enables a person to defer instant gratification for long-term gain. It's sometimes called the 'moral policeman' because it helps us to make sensible decisions.

So, a parent might fail to understand why their teenage daughter is Facetiming her boyfriend till 3am on the night before a GCSE exam, but the reality is that the daughter probably hasn't thought through the consequences. Her brain isn't fully developed yet.

Secondly, peer pressure is a huge factor influencing young people. If there's a group of lads gathered round a computer looking at porn, it's going to be very difficult for one of them to say no. The need for a young person to fit in and be accepted is massive.[11]

In this case it's really the parents – our children – who need our prayers. Our job is to pray for and support them in any way we can, and educate ourselves at least enough to be able to talk with our grandchildren should the occasion arise and hold our own if we need to. It's so tempting to turn our backs on what we don't understand.

Praying for children who are being brought up to know Jesus and become familiar with the Bible, and who are part of a church community, however flawed it may be, is a deep pleasure, and often our prayers for such families will be full of thanksgiving. Susie says that one of her greatest pleasures is hearing her son sing the same bedtime songs to his children that she sang to him as a child. She writes:

> Both sets of grandchildren (nine months and nine years) have Christian parents. We try to reinforce what our children are doing, but also to make sure the parents are the chief faith guides… We pray for our children, for wisdom in bringing the grandchildren up to know, love and serve the Lord. We pray daily that God would build the character of Christ in them. We also pray for our own relationship with the respective families, for wisdom in relating to them without interfering or counteracting the way they choose to bring the children up.
>
> As the child of a vicar myself, I am very aware of the pressures on the grandchildren whose dad is also a clergyman. I think this makes me particularly aware of the pressures and expectations upon them, motivating my prayers for the protection of their faith.

For those of us, however, whose children don't share our faith or who have left church, our prayers for them and our grandchildren may be more like those of Jeremiah, the weeping prophet:

> Since my people are crushed, I am crushed; I mourn, and horror grips me... Oh, that my head were a spring of water and my eyes a fountain of tears! I would weep day and night for the slain of my people... You who are my Comforter in sorrow, my heart is faint within me.[12]

A reminder: although this is how we may see them – as crushed and slain, metaphorically speaking – they, of course, probably feel absolutely fine and at peace with all their choices, and, as we've already noted, it is of huge importance that we respect this, and that they know we respect them. What I'm getting at here is that if we feel overwhelmed and despairing, the proper place to take this is to God himself.

Writing about betrayal from a friend, David says:

> As for me, I call to God, and the Lord saves me. Evening, morning and noon I cry out in distress, and he hears my voice... Cast your cares on the Lord and he will sustain you... but as for me I trust in you.[13]

There are many patterns we can follow to help us pray, from using a simple acrostic, such as ACTS (adoration, confession, thanksgiving, supplication), to praying through the Lord's Prayer phrase by phrase, or even word by word, to praying through the names of Jesus.[14] Likewise there are many devotional books with a daily reading that can jumpstart our prayers. For me one of the most fruitful ways of praying for many years has been turning the words of the Bible itself into prayer. It takes time and practice to become skilled at this, but it's a reassuring form of prayer, not least because you can be sure that God agrees with your prayers, since the Bible is the expression of his will:

> This is the confidence we have in approaching God: that if we ask anything according to his will, he hears us. And if we know that he hears us – whatever we ask – we know that we have what we asked of him.[15]

We should note that the word 'now' is not in this verse. No time frame is specified, just an equation. One thing ensures the other. We tend to be conditioned by our online culture that delivers at the touch of a button, so that any delay in answers to our prayers can be seen as a negative response. But God is not a cashpoint or a click away.

James reminds us how easy it is to ask with our own plans in mind rather than God's: 'When you ask, you do not receive, because you ask with wrong motives, that you may spend what you get on your pleasures.'[16] And he's not talking only about spending money. At the same time he encourages us to ask: 'You do not have because you do not ask God.'[17]

The apostle Peter writes, 'With the Lord a day is like a thousand years, and a thousand years are like a day.'[18] This is what C.S. Lewis so brilliantly conveys in 'The Chronicles of Narnia', when an adventure in Narnia that covers years or even centuries turns out to have taken five minutes when the children are transported back to earth.

I hope that this will encourage you to keep praying, though the wait may be long. The parable of the persistent widow was told 'to show Jesus' disciples that they should always pray and not give up'.[19] And the apostle Paul exhorts the Galatians, 'Let us not become weary in doing good, for at the proper time we will reap a harvest if we do not give up.'[20] There's the time factor again.

A dear friend often reminds me that she had to wait until her son was 50 years old for him to discover Jesus. Much more famously, St Augustine's mother, Monica, prayed steadfastly for her son, who at the age of 16 was living a life far from God. He had fathered a child and joined a heretical group. Monica persisted in prayer for him for 19 years, often coming before God and weeping for her son. In desperation she asked a bishop to speak to Augustine, but he refused her request, saying, 'Leave him alone for a time… only pray to God for him… Go thy way and God bless thee, for it is not possible that the son of these tears should perish.' Monica prayed passionately for many years and lived to see her son come back to God and go on to become one of the leading bishops of the fourth century and join the company of the church fathers. His writings remain a primary theological source of learning today.[21]

Our tears will never be wasted. David asks God to 'list my tears on your scroll'. Another translation says, 'put my tears in your bottle'.[22] This refers to the ancient custom of putting precious tears shed in mourning in a small phial that would be placed in the tomb of the deceased. Just as he said to Hezekiah, God says to us, 'I have heard your prayer and seen your tears.'[23]

Let's take two scriptures to demonstrate the practice of praying the Bible. Why don't you treat this as an exercise and do it as you read (changing the gender of the pronouns if necessary). First, using Psalm 1 to pray for a child in a Christian home:

'Blessed is the one who does not walk in step with the wicked' – 'Lord, there's much evil in our country, all sorts of malign as well as benign influences. Please help [the child's name] to see the difference between the two, which is often so difficult and subtle. There's so much out there in the guise of good that yet leads to unhealthy thinking. Please protect her from coming under influences that will lead her away from you and your people.'

'or stand in the way that sinners take' – 'Lord, please guide and shape the company she keeps. Lead her to like-minded friends who will strengthen her faith but give her also friends who don't know you; help her to love people for who they are, not with the goal of changing them.'

'*or sit in the company of mockers*' – 'Lord, you showed no dis-crimination when you walked on this earth, and you show none now. Please fill her with your Spirit so that she will truly be inclusive in her love, even as a child, and be able to resist the delicious temptation of criticism and mockery. Help her especially in the playground. Let her be '*like a tree planted by streams of water*'.[24] Let her be fruitful and not become dry. Lord, lead her deep into the stream of your word, so that her mind will be healthy. Lord, I long for her to grow up to make good decisions that lead to life and flourishing.'

The second half of Psalm 1 is trickier, but we don't have to pray the whole Bible. In Psalm 131, David says, 'I do not concern myself with great matters or things too wonderful for me,'[25] and we might add, 'or things too complicated for me, such as understanding exactly how we might qualify for the wicked camp'.

As a second example, we might pray from Ephesians, again according to the family situation. Paul is writing to the new church in Ephesus. So for another grandchild we might pray with thanks from chapter 1, 'Thank you that you've provided every spiritual blessing for [*the child's name*]. Thank you that you've chosen him for yourself. Please keep his faith safe and alive and help him navigate the challenges he's facing now at school and is bound to face in the future.'[26]

Although Paul's letter is written to Christians, we can take the words and pray them for grandchildren who may be growing up outside a church or Christian community context. For another grandchild, perhaps a teenager who's beginning the normal process of separating from parents and working out who he is becoming:

> Father, show him how wide and long and high and deep your love is; show him you care about him more than anyone else does, much more than us or even his parents; show him that your love isn't restrictive, and that you delight in the person you've made him. Show him the immeasurable dimensions of your love, Lord. You can do that![27]

We can pray with tears, pray with persistence and pray expectantly. As has been said, it'll all be all right in the end, and if it's not all right, it's not the end.

In our prayers for them, it's easy to focus on the giants that our grandchildren may be facing. We should beware of our imaginations wildly exaggerating what we fear may be the situation of any particular child or family. The story of David facing Goliath is an inspiring picture of choosing to trust God in the face of something huge and intimidating. As we pray for our grandchildren, we must fix our gaze on the one to whom we pray, not on any giants, and remind ourselves, as David reminded the Israelites, 'the battle is the Lord's'.[28]

Our most heartfelt cry to God will be for their love and knowledge of Jesus to grow continually deeper and richer, or for them to return to him, to come home. But there are many wonderful things we can pray for them along the way. As Jo Swinney and Katharine Hill write:

> We can pray God's blessing on every aspect of their lives. We can pray scripture over them. We can pray for Christian friends and people of influence to come into their lives; that God would use every opportunity to speak to them; and that their eyes would be opened to see the things of God. We can pray on our own in the secret place, with our spouse or our friends. We can pray in the morning or evening, for minutes or hours. We can pray while doing chores, we can pray in the car, on the bus, on the phone. We can take any and every opportunity to pray.[29]

Praying *with* them

Jane says of praying with her grandchildren:

> The under-fives seem very focused on simple, everyday things. They say a thank-you prayer each night. When we are there,

they often say, 'Thank you, God, that Grandma and Grandad came today and brought a yummy tea (or Grandma's books),' or, 'Thank you, God, we had strawberries for tea.' A reminder to us of the blessings of simple things and of simplicity.

Much more important than the content of our prayers with them is the hope that our little grandchildren will know Jesus is real and listening, and that talking to him will gradually grow their friendship with him. Isabel says:

We pray daily for each grandchild, and often I pray with them, especially if they are going through something difficult. This usually happens at bedtime, or sometimes at meals, but with the older ones (from about seven up), really any time can work.

For children who have grown up in the company of Jesus, as it were, this can bring great security. Isabel says:

I think the fact that Jesus is alive and real, that it's possible to really know him – and not just talk to him when in trouble, but to listen to him and talk to him all the time as they do with us or their parents – makes a lot of difference. A four-year-old grandson once said to me, 'Do you know, Granny, even if you go through the shadow of death, Jesus will be with you? Not just Friday or Saturday, *all* the time. You're never scared; you're never even lonely.' I'm sure he took the first part of that on trust! But the loving presence and protection of God had always been the natural context of his life.

Perhaps the fact that this particular child spent several of his early years in Kenya, and had to travel a long and dangerous road for sports matches from his rural school to Nairobi, helped make his pronouncements real and rooted.

Helen has some inspiring ideas:

One of the privileges of being a grandparent, with all the accrued wisdom and hindsight we have received, is to pray for them. I used to speak the name of Jesus over our children's cots when they were tiny, so they'd be familiar with his name as they grew older. And I did the same over our grandchildren's cots. We, being retired, pray daily for them, and as different needs arise, such as schooling or friendship, night terrors or anxieties, we pray about particular circumstances and feelings. I keep a prayer diary for my grandchildren, and they or their parents give me specific requests.

Praying with grandchildren can also be an opportunity for gentle teaching. Helen says:

Once when I asked two of my granddaughters what I could pray for them, one gave me a long list of things, mostly involving friends at school, and the other said, 'I have such a good life, I can't think of anything.' After a pause, she added, 'There is something. There's a boy in my class who's a bit mean. Could you pray he gets ill?' We both laughed, and she reluctantly agreed that God probably wouldn't answer that prayer!

It goes without saying that this assumes that the parents of our grandchildren are comfortable with us praying with them; if this is not the case, we just have to take a deep breath and remind ourselves of our commitment to respect our children's choices. Our prayers will have to be for them rather than with them, and we'll have to wait until they're old enough to ask their own questions of us – and we pray that they do.

Some of us will find that we do more praying for our grandchildren than talking to them about matters of faith. But we should never give up praying, because God hears us. As the psalmist says, 'All my longings lie open before you.'[30] Here's Chris' story of a grandparent's prayers answered:

As a child I was aware that my grandmother was a committed Christian and that the rest of us weren't. When I was nine, Grandma came to live with us for a while, and that's when I realised that she was also a woman of prayer; and because her prayers were loud enough to be heard through her closed door, I came to know that much of the time she was praying for us!

Two years later, Grandma died after suffering several strokes. At her thanksgiving service I remember being struck by the sincerity of the people, especially their sense of hope and joy. I decided after the service that I wouldn't volunteer to go back, but that if my mum asked me to go, I would say yes. Sure enough, the next week she did ask, and so I joined her. Six weeks later, my mother recommitted her life to Christ, and both I and my sister had also become Christians. Thirty-six long years later, kneeling beside his bed on his 73rd birthday, my dad gave his life to Christ.

My grandmother didn't live to see her daughter recommit her life to Christ, nor her granddaughter and son-in-law become Christians, nor me become a Christian worker and then a minister. But God answered her fervent, sincere and rather loud prayers, by quite literally bringing redemption to us through her death.

I once met the rector of a well-known large and thriving church, who told me that although he had barely seen his grandparents throughout his childhood, he developed a strong bond with his grandfather during his student years and attributes much of his spiritual understanding and passion for Christ to the prayers, time and input of this grandparent. If, for the reasons we've looked at, you're not able to see much of your grandchildren, please don't give up praying for them daily; you're building a deposit of prayer that will one day bear fruit.

As the rain and the snow come down from heaven, and do not return to it without watering the earth and making it bud and flourish, so that it yields seed for the sower and bread for the eater, so is my word that goes out from my mouth: it will not return to me empty, but will accomplish what I desire and achieve the purpose for which I sent it.[31]

As well as the reassurance in this passage, it's a great encouragement to us to turn the very words of the Bible into our prayers.

You may be reading this as someone who came to faith recently, perhaps after your children have flown the nest, and may be thinking, 'How can I ever catch up?' Or you may be wishing with a pang that you'd thought of some of these things when your own children were little. But the kingdom of God is not one of first come, first served; rather it's an upside-down kingdom, in which 'the last will be first, and the first will be last'.[32] If hope and resolution are rising up within you, be encouraged – the Lord loves a tender heart that turns to him, and he can 'repay you for the years the locusts have eaten'.[33]

12

What about me? Soul-keeping

Your statutes are my heritage forever; they are the joy of my heart.
PSALM 119:111

Eros will have naked bodies, friendship naked personalities.
C.S. Lewis[1]

Trampolines are the swing sets of the 21st century and cover our country like giant sieves. Hardly a garden that ever sees children is without one, and trampoline parks have now sprung up across the country, which has created a phenomenon called Trampoline World. Trust me – go online and check!

I try to be a game granny, who will join in and play with my grandchildren, but my most recent trampoline experience (*not* in a trampoline park) reminded me that joining in should be selective and demonstrate wisdom. The grandchildren, of course, shrieked with delight, deliberately throwing me off balance as I hurtled round.

Just as we can lose our balance physically, we can lose it emotionally, mentally or spiritually, and by the time we become grandparents we're likely to have taken a few knocks, some taking longer than others to recover from. We've talked a lot about navigating the joys and the trials of being grandparents. In this chapter, I want to explore the question of how we look after ourselves – soul-keeping as well as body-keeping – in this business of being Christian grandparents.

We all know the subtle pressure to resist ageing, which comes from the media and advertising, as well as from within ourselves to some degree. It's hard to remain unaffected and free of corporate consciousness. Even my dentist's waiting room greets me with a huge picture of a 60-something displaying a perfect set of gleaming white gnashers, a picture designed to persuade me that I'd feel so much better if I signed up for implants. Not a chance! I have a dear friend who did and has been eating pureed food for months.

We know really that looking after our bodies isn't primarily about trying to adjust them to fit a cultural demand or expectation, but about healthy eating, exercise, getting enough sleep and including rest in our schedules. We can ask ourselves what cultural expectation we are trying to live up to as grandparents. Are we helicopter grandparents, unable to stop keeping our eye on our offspring? Or are we heroic grandparents, rushing to the rescue when the alarm sounds? To my shame, I have fallen into this trap on occasion, motivated, of course, by love and care; however, not only can we intrude in this way, but we can also overspend our resources so that our physical capacity to bless our families well is diminished and our help not available when it's really needed.

In the same way we can overextend ourselves emotionally, because we care about our families more than anyone. Just as a car that is driven faster must refuel more frequently, so the more intense our emotional lives are, the more quickly we can become depleted and need re-energising. So how can we take care of ourselves as grandparents and make sure that we regularly refuel?

First, we must recognise and accept that we are growing older. This may seem obvious, but despite the increasing number of elderly people in the population, and the regular warnings of a care crisis, as a culture we are wilfully blind to the reality of growing old. It won't happen to me, we think. The pharmaceutical and cosmetic industries reinforce our refusal to entertain the concept, and so we journey blithely on, unprepared for anything that the passage of time might bring us.

Here are wise grandparent words from my mother: 'Life's a bit like a play: at a certain point you're centre stage, and that's where you are now. We're not centre stage any more, but moving towards the wings.' Most of us have a deep, if subconscious, desire to be permanently centre stage. But we'll do well if we don't resist the move towards the wings. Part of accepting the slow advance of age is recognising 'the gift of limits'.[2] We have physical limits, like mine on the trampoline, but we also have limits to what we can carry emotionally, and if we are carrying a heavy emotional burden in our family, we would be wise to look for help. There are times for most of us when we need to recover our inner stability, for example, if some unexpected news has knocked us off balance. This is what emotional maturity is: not thinking I can manage by myself but recognising my need of help.

As grandparents, we desire nothing more than to give generous and inexhaustible support to our grandchildren and their families, but we must also receive support. Some of that support will come from others but some of it we must provide for ourselves – putting on our own oxygen mask before helping someone else with theirs.

At a buffet meal, whether at an all-you-can-eat diner, a wedding or a party, there is no control on the amount we can consume – no control except our own, that is. We're responsible for making our own diet healthy. As with the physical, so with the spiritual: we're responsible for our Bible diet. 'Man shall not live on bread alone, but on every word that comes from the mouth of God.'[3] There's a veritable smorgasbord of Bible reading notes and apps out there to help us with this, and surely something to suit every temperament and preference. I use one or two, but for me by far the deepest stream flows through the practice of *lectio divina*,[4] which is Latin for 'divine reading' and means meditating on the scriptures. The practice began in early monasteries as a way to 'feast on the word'. It's like wine-tasting or slowly sucking a butterscotch – it's a rich vein of nourishment, continually unveiling meaning and expanding our understanding.

We've given lots of attention to praying for and with our grandchildren, but here we're thinking about our personal time alone with God. Relational familiarity comes from time spent together and mutual listening. One of the most fruitful – and indispensable – forms of soul care is meeting with God, ideally every day, even for a few minutes if that's all we have. We can listen to him through his word and tell him our concerns, anxieties and hopes about the day ahead or the day behind us. And we can thank him. Whatever our circumstances, there will always be something we can thank God for. Even at that time of greatest loss in my life, when Samuel died and all the strength drained out of our bodies and the colour out of our world, we had things to thank our Father for: close friends; surrogate parents (we were in the United States, away from our own); a church community that loved in deed as well as word. Daily dwelling like this develops the most priceless relationship we will ever have, which is our friendship with God.

Thomas Aquinas made friendship with God the basis for all our understanding of love, both for God and neighbour. You may be surprised to read that the root meaning of the word 'intimacy' has to do with friendship rather than sexuality, as is commonly understood in our culture. The Latin *intimus* means close friend, and the Collins dictionary defines a friend as: 'A person known well to another, and regarded with liking, affection and loyalty; an intimate.' Adam walking with God before the fall conveys this sense of intimate friendship. The interaction between God and Abraham likewise speaks of friendship: 'Shall I hide from Abraham what I am about to do?'[5] Here we see marks of friendship – trust, confidence and revelation. Moses is also portrayed as a friend of God: 'The Lord would speak to Moses face to face, as one speaks to a friend.'[6]

In John 15, Jesus instructs the disciples to remain in his love and keep his commandments, telling them that this will bring them overflowing, amazing joy. He promotes them from servants to friends, saying, 'I no longer call you servants, because a servant does not know his master's business. Instead, I have called you friends.'[7] They are now on the inside loop, in the know. This is what real friendship is.

In building our lifelong friendship with God, I recommend keeping a journal. Moments of deep connection come from time to time, moments in which we sense a significance beyond today, perhaps direction for the future, a promise for our life, an encouragement for the soul. It makes real sense to record such moments, because tomorrow's tide will ineluctably flow in, erasing the writing in the sand.

Another source of input is taking a retreat[8] from time to time, to complement our daily spiritual disciplines and help us maintain them. It's like stretching our daily coffee break time with God to a long and lingering meal. Being alone with God regenerates the depths of our soul and slows our breathing. How long you or I can stretch it to depends entirely on our personal circumstances, but anything from the inside of a day to two or three whole days away will surprise you with joy, I promise you. Then there are hardcore retreats, such as week-long silent retreats or an Ignatian 30-day retreat. As grandparents it's possible that these latter forms will not be completely unthinkable for us.

Incidentally, retreats do not need to break the bank; there are inexpensive retreat centres, and one of the great blessings of belonging to a church is the extravagant sharing among its members. When we lived in France, a couple from another church spontaneously offered us the use of their Normandy country cottage, which became a beloved place of retreat and encounter for us.

Spiritual directors are increasingly sought after today. The title is a misnomer, since far from telling you what to do, a spiritual director accompanies you on your life journey with God. This is beautifully captured in the eighth-century Coptic icon *Christ and Abbot Mena*,[9] which illustrates tenderness and care. The beauty of this time (usually a disciplined hour) is that it's a space for you. Unlike most of our relationships, which demand mutual interest and listening, you have no obligation to care for your spiritual director in any way and can freely talk out your soul and state. Paradoxically, often these sessions do lead to the forming of a friendship, which is an unplanned bonus, and like being given a present you don't expect.

Let's pause here and reflect honestly about our spiritual disciplines. How about taking an appointment with the 'Wonderful Counsellor, Mighty God, Everlasting Father, Prince of Peace'?[10]

We must help ourselves, but we also need the help of others. A spouse or partner will often be the nearest and closest support, but while marriage is a primary friendship it's also a journey of discovery:

> A marriage is not a joining of two worlds, but an abandoning of two worlds in order that one new one might be formed... It is a vocation to total abandonment... in getting married one espouses... an unimaginable breadth of possibility.[11]

Our spouse can't be expected to meet all our needs. As the years pass, both parties will change and so will their needs, and we can't be a psychologist or a counsellor to our spouse. While we may come to need help from either of these professionals for a time, we will always need the support of our friends, as will those of us who are single for whatever reason, perhaps even more so.

The psychiatrist Paul Tournier writes of the vital importance of preparing for retirement and transitioning into it slowly:

> The older one is, the more value one places on human dialogue. With advancing age one begins to ask all sorts of questions that previously seemed unimportant. Death is approaching

in all its mystery. He has been a success in his job – has he been a success in his life? It's not a good idea to turn over such problems all on one's own.[12]

Yet, as Tournier continues:

People are reluctant to talk about old age and death because they are afraid of emotion, and they willingly avoid the things they feel most emotional about, though these are the very things they most need to talk about.[13]

Wendy says:

Many grandparents become a single grandparent, and that is the aspect from which I tell my tale. My grandchildren became a part of my resource when initially widowed – they gave me hope for life beyond my newly found 'status'. After my husband's death, Jesus' words 'Today is enough'[14] became my mantra to live in the present; today is a gift, open it and enjoy it.

Facing such loss is difficult. Face it one must, though, to journey on through – not over or under or around but through, and healing comes with the help of friends and family who journey alongside.

Writing things down can be helpful, and encouragement is encouraging! What's extremely unhelpful is others thinking they know what's best for me or how I feel… My family, friends and 'heart buddies' all help me see that fullness of life is possible despite being alone.

My first port of call, echoing Wendy's accent on this, would be friends with a capital F. Not Facebook friends, not acquaintances, not church friends – friends who happen to go to the same or another church, yes, but that's quite a different thing. Even if we are married, our well-being is enhanced by having good friends, both of the same and of the opposite sex. Loneliness is a modern-day plague, despite more ways of connecting with others than ever before.

> What most strikes me... is the full force of the restlessness, the loneliness and the tension that holds so many people. The conversations I had today were about spiritual survival. So many of my friends feel overwhelmed by the many demands made on them; few feel the inner peace and joy they so much desire.[15]

The internet, which opens the door to a myriad of connections, can eventually isolate us and stunt our remaining relationships. Since the publication in 2000 of Robert Putnam's famous book *Bowling Alone*,[16] which drew attention to the problem, the breakdown of community and civic society has steadily continued, and, today, going to a bowling alley alone – Putnam's central symbol of 'social capital deficit' – would actually be definitively social, compared to the 'bowling' (and host of other pseudo-social acts) that we do online. If we are city dwellers, 'we cram into buses or the underground, in solid, silent masses, in which the promiscuity of our bodies is equalled only by the solitude of our spirits'.[17]

The dissolution of local community, and technology that permits us to construct a fantasy or isolated world, are certainly contributing factors to the plague of loneliness, and many are wandering in the wasteland of our strongly individualist culture – the signposts of old have been taken down, and we can't find our way around anymore. Am I just talking about the millennials? About our grandchildren? No. I think many of us who are baby boomers are also floundering as we try to adjust to the tsunami of changes that are sweeping the western world.

Articles and statistics analysing social isolation abound in the media and on the internet. One of the most tragic and most telling is that over half of all people over 75 live alone.[18] Loneliness is a bigger problem than simply an emotional experience, because research shows that loneliness and social isolation are harmful to our health. As a risk factor for early death, lacking social connections is comparable to smoking 15 cigarettes a day, and it affects us more seriously than well-known risk factors, such as obesity and physical inactivity. Grandparents we may be, but investing in the real people who are our friends in real time and in real places is crucial to our well-being. Quite apart from the health benefits, friends offer mutual support in our grandparenting.

True friendship is becoming increasingly rare. The advent of the internet may be one cause, but another is that getting to know a person takes a long time and demands a lot of investment. Today we talk a lot about investing in relationships. Investment, of course, is a banking term, but we've hijacked the term because we know instinctively that we can't accrue interest on a relationship unless we invest in it. What does this mean? It means time, which is far and away our most precious commodity, though you would never know it from the way we treat it. We waste it, we idle it away and we run through our days from pillar to post; we forget that of all the commodities available to us, time is the only one we can never replace.

As today draws to a close, take a moment to consider this and reflect on what sort of a day it's been. Take 15 precious minutes to do the Examen.[19] If we were more aware of the uniqueness of each day, we might be more conscious of how we spend it, but as it is, we often miss the present altogether because our minds are racing anxiously back to the past or forward into the future. If only we could be here now. Here. Now.

Today many of us are still working when we are grandparents, so have more demands on our time than former generations did. While making our families a priority, we can inadvertently short-change ourselves on our friends. So what are we looking for in friends? All of us need friends with whom we can be vulnerable, open up our innermost struggles and wounds, and unashamedly ask for help.

Perhaps, particularly as Christian grandparents, we feel an inner pressure for our families to fulfil the expectations of others – or of ourselves. We can hide where we are really at, because somehow we feel ashamed of what isn't going to plan in our families. This has been called 'broken secrecy'.

A true friend is one who provides a place of safety, where we can reveal who we are and acknowledge the darker parts of our history. If we can do friendship well, our friendships will be one of the most important sources of help to us as we battle our demons and pursue Christlikeness. C.S. Lewis, in *The Four Loves*, describes the love of friendship – *philia*.[20] *Philia* has a long history of association with love for God, that is, *caritas* (charity) and *agape* (sacrificial love). Plato and Aristotle, among other philosophers, along with the church fathers and the mystics, all had things to say about friendship. Augustine writes:

> Particularly when I am worn out by the upsets of the world, I cast myself without reservation on the love of those who are especially close to me. I know I can safely entrust my thoughts and considerations to those who are aflame with Christian love and have become faithful friends to me.[21]

Proverbs echoes Augustine's thought: 'There is a friend who sticks closer than a brother.'[22] C.S. Lewis writes:

> In friendship… we think we have chosen our peers. In reality a few years' difference in the dates of our births, a few more miles between certain houses, the choice of one university instead of another… the accident of a topic being raised or not raised at a first meeting – any of these chances might have kept us apart. But, for a Christian, there are, strictly speaking, no chances. A secret master of ceremonies has been at work. Christ, who said to the disciples, 'Ye have not chosen me, but I have chosen you,' can truly say to every group of Christian friends, 'You have not chosen one another but I have chosen you for one another.'

Friendship is… the instrument by which God reveals to each of us the beauties of others.[23]

Real friendship takes precious, irreplaceable time, so if we aspire to deep friendships, we must reckon with the cost but know that every minute given to such friendships is worth its time in gold. Proverbs puts it like this: 'A friend loves at all times.'[24]

Real friendship demands the courage to know and be known. As a friendship grows in depth and familiarity, it's inevitable that our flaws (and theirs) will become apparent. This is the point at which so many potential friendships flounder and fade, but if we face and accept their flaws (and ours) and keep pressing in to the friendship, resisting the temptation to let fear make us back out of our commitment to it, we'll be rewarded with something true and invaluable that gives great joy.

Clearly there's a level of friendship and intimacy that must be intuitively reached before we can permit mutual challenging and intimate questioning, but real friendships include these things. Proverbs speaks often of the wisdom of accepting discipline and correction:

Whoever heeds life-giving correction will be at home among the wise. Those who disregard discipline despise themselves, but the one who heeds correction gains understanding.[25]

And we need friends who love us so much they're ready to risk offending us: 'Wounds from a friend can be trusted; but an enemy multiplies kisses.'[26]

In a real friendship, it's safe to confront and disagree. Such a moment will often determine whether or not the friendship is real and lasting, and will lead to forgiveness, which in turn leads to healing – and so the friendship becomes deeper and more secure and weathered. Real friendships survive disagreement, something clearly illustrated in the relationship between God and Abraham, as the scriptures confirm the friendship well beyond their discussion about Sodom and Gomorrah in Genesis 18.[27]

It wouldn't be right to pretend that making friends is risk-free. 'Do what you came for, friend'[28] – this deep friendship between Jesus and Judas is very challenging for us as Christians, because it fulfilled all the criteria for an intimate friendship yet proved unsafe. Ultimately, we can't rule out the risk of betrayal, but investing in deep friendship is still worth the risk.

> To love at all is to be vulnerable. Love anything, and your heart will certainly be wrung and possibly be broken. If you want to make sure of keeping it intact, you must give your heart to no one, not even to an animal.[29]

Although Christians enjoy the extra dimension of shared faith in friendship, all these principles are universal and apply irrespective of a person's stance on faith. We have very close, long-standing friends who wouldn't call themselves Christians, but whom we love as we love all our friends, and in whom we confide with great confidence. They, too, bear the *imago dei*.

Friendship is binary, whether on social media or in a social setting. We may have a party with 100 friends, at which we may make a speech, but the only way that any of the friendships present at the party will deepen or grow will be face-to-face. We may be at a wedding or other event, where we have friendships with a number of people, maybe many, but the only way any of the friendships present will grow or deepen is through face-to-face exchanges. Every Sunday I will be in the company of several hundred people, often twice in the day. But I will only have three or four friendship-deepening exchanges. Facebook may be a good networking medium, but it's not really a good friend-making medium – not least because real 'un-friending' is a lot more complicated than the click of a button.

Jesus supremely modelled having special friends, but he had many different levels of friends: twelve disciples, among whom three were his intimates; many female friends; and 72 disciples who were sent out on mission. Unsurprisingly research indicates the number of close friendships we can healthily sustain to be about twelve. As Proverbs says, 'A man of many companions may come to ruin, but there is a friend who sticks closer than a brother.'[30]

As grandparents, we're part of a community (or communities) wider than just our family, and part of the community of people who share our streets, shops and services. But within all this we need intimate friendships.

Real friendship crosses every barrier, divide and generation; I have friends in their late 80s, friends in their 30s and 40s, and my children are also my friends. Real friends should be allowed to see our tears as well as hear our laughter. Jesus modelled vulnerability in a variety of contexts, but it was in the garden of Gethsemane that he openly showed his need of his friends.

> When we honestly ask ourselves which person in our lives mean the most to us, we often find that it is those who, instead of giving advice, solutions, or cures, have chosen rather to share our pain and touch our wounds with a warm and tender hand. The friend who can be silent with us in a moment of despair or confusion, who can stay with us in an hour of grief and bereavement, who can tolerate not knowing, not curing, not healing and face with us the reality of our powerlessness, that is a friend who cares.[31]

> I am struck by how sharing our weakness and difficulties is more nourishing to others than sharing our qualities and successes.[32]

Apart from the supreme example of Jesus, the Bible offers models of deep friendship that we can draw from. Some of these are explicit, such as David's friendship with Jonathan, Naomi's friendship with Ruth and Paul's friendship with Timothy, and others we perceive only on closer inspection. Paul clearly had a number of close friends – Priscilla and Aquila, Epaphras, Onesimus and more besides.

Friendship is vastly bigger and wider-reaching than marriage. Jesus supremely demonstrates that marriage is not the only solution to aloneness, and the truth is that marriage is temporal, while friendship is eternal. We need to demythologise marriage. So many marriages are places of great loneliness and pain, and, in our lonely culture, we must recognise that the married and the unmarried need each other, in the same way that the young need the old and the old the young.

At least twice a year I travel to meet two beloved friends with whom I can open my heart about literally anything, except our husbands – though I'm certain that if any of our marriages was at risk, we would go there too. We cry, pray, laugh and talk together for 36 hours or so, often sitting round the breakfast table in our pyjamas for hours. Importantly, we can absorb disagreement – there are things we disagree quite profoundly on, but our love for each other is decades-old and deep.

I wonder how you would describe your friendships? As we change with the passing seasons, so our friendships wax and wane, but I believe God offers all of us a few lifelong friends. I hope that, like me, you can testify to such friendships, but if the painful truth – and sometimes a thought can trigger physical pain – is that there's a friendship vacuum in your life, my prayer is that reading this will prompt you to take action, even if in the first instance it involves simply humbling yourself to admit the truth to one person. It may be that you are realising that you do sometimes feel lonely, and you are asking yourself, 'Who actually are my friends?' Are they really the kind of friends we've been talking about here?

Well, put the book down for a minute and start by having a friendship-deepening time with God. Talk to him about this. No more burying of ghosts. Tell him about friendships that have gone wrong or withered through lack of investment; tell him about friendships that started with great promise but have become superficial, and you are wondering whether to kickstart them again or gracefully let them go. Then he'll show you what to do.

As you make that choice to give some time to God, tell him that your desire is to revitalise your friendship with him, too.

Before I leave you, I have a last little story.

Arriving at their home, I find my nearly six-year-old granddaughter Esme bouncing off the walls with excitement and dressed in a glamorous outfit recently worn to a family wedding. Round her neck dangles a pair of binoculars thoughtfully provided by her mother. She chatters incessantly as I change, and soon we are in the taxi and on our way – to the Royal Opera House to see *The Nutcracker*. But the chattering has ceased, as the scary realisation that Mummy and Daddy are no longer present sinks in, so I put my arm round her and give a sort of running commentary about our progress to reassure her that all is well, which it is, and soon we arrive at the stage door and ring the bell.

Why the stage door? Because in one of those wonderful 'coincidences' of life, I met one of the Royal Opera House ballet corps dancers a couple of months earlier, who on learning that I would be at a performance with Esme immediately offered us a backstage tour before the show. So, here we are, grandmother and granddaughter equally excited!

Fine-featured and beautiful, with a graceful, floating walk, Ashley embodies everyone's vision of a ballet dancer. But she's also very friendly and welcomes us warmly, putting an over-awed little girl at ease. We set off through the maze of corridors, the kind of village behind the auditorium of this majestic London landmark, and are led from room to room – the tutu room; the ballet-shoe room; the make-up and dressing room, where each dancer has their dressing table; and the gym, where that evening's Clara is practising alone, and time stands still as we watch. Ashley shows us hundreds of costumes: great heavy jewel-encrusted robes and dresses as well as the gossamer and gauze of tutus; we see crowns – Ashley gently lowers a great crown on to Esme's head in front of the mirror – and fabulous wigs. But the best is yet to come, for as we arrive back at the stage door, Ashley says, 'I've got a little present for you, Esme,' and seemingly from nowhere (I certainly haven't seen her pick it up) produces a bag, which Esme opens to reveal a pair of Ashley's ballet shoes no longer fit for purpose, but still beautiful – and covered with cast members' signatures!

The rest of the evening lives up to the pre-event, and Esme manages to stay awake right till the end of this most enchanting of all ballets. Safely home after a sleepy journey, Esme suddenly rediscovers her lost voice. For a strong extrovert, she had been uncharacteristically quiet all evening, but I know that like me she will never forget our magical experience.

Sometimes life brings us times of great joy, and for me this is one of them, and will be a treasured memory that never fades. But more than that, it reminds me that life brings wonderful times, as well as dark times, light as well as dark – and that light is more powerful than darkness.

We've travelled together through all sorts of aspects of life for a grandparent who follows Jesus Christ, and considered our calling to be faithful to him, and unfailingly loving towards our families. Like me, you will have had your 'Nutcracker' moments, maybe much more simple or homely. The nugget of gold in these times is not the place or the event, but the connection. And that can be given anywhere, as deeply in a few seconds as a few hours. You and I know there will be easy times and hard times in our families, and I hope and pray that like a skilled mountaineer, you've found handholds for your ascent as you've read. I leave you with my prayer that your days and months may be bejewelled with these kindnesses of God as you journey with him, and that you will always hold out hope and love to your children and grandchildren – and maybe even great-grandchildren.

Don't ever forget the truth that he will never leave you nor forsake you:

> Whoever dwells in the shelter of the Most High will rest in the shadow of the Almighty. I will say of the Lord, 'He is my refuge and my fortress, my God in whom I trust…' Under his wings you will find refuge; his faithfulness will be your shield.[33]

Appendices

A Patterns of prayer

Praying the Lord's Prayer

Our Father in heaven
Begin with intimate worship and thanking God for his fatherhood.

Hallowed be your name
Continue to worship and meditate with a daily hallowing of the name of God.

Your kingdom come, your will be done, on earth as it is in heaven
Pray for healing and deliverance, church planting, missionary activity, the nations, the care of creation and rescue of the earth, the conversion of the lost, and the rule of God into different parts of society and into the world around you.

Give us today our daily bread
John Wimber said, 'Give us tomorrow's bread today.'[1] We can pray that the provision of the kingdom flows into our lives today: money needed for projects or survival, jobs for the unemployed, spiritual food for us and for our children.

And forgive us our sins as we forgive those who sin against us
Take time to ask the Holy Spirit to reveal what may not please him in your life and confess it. Then make confession on behalf of the church, community and nation. Study Nehemiah 1 and 9 for this practice.

And do not bring us to a time of trial, but deliver us from evil
Strong spiritual warfare against the forces of darkness is important. A praying church needs to grow in authority and discernment in this area.

For yours is the kingdom, the power and the glory, for ever and ever
Be sure to end a time of private or corporate prayer with praise, which can put things back into a right perspective.

Amen.

Praying the names of God

Names of God from the Old Testament
- Yahweh Hesed – Loving God (Exodus 34:6)
- Yahweh Tsebaaoth – The Lord of hosts (1 Samuel 17:45)
- Yahweh Elyon – Lord Most High (Psalm 7:8)
- Yahweh Jireh – The Lord will provide (Genesis 22:14)
- Yahweh Roï – The Lord my shepherd (Psalm 23:1)
- Yahweh Nissi – The Lord is my banner (Exodus 17:15)
- Yahweh Shalom – The Lord is peace (Judges 6:24)
- Yahweh Shammah – The Lord is there (Ezekiel 48:35)
- Yahweh Tsidkenou – The Lord our righteous saviour (Jeremiah 23:6)
- Yahweh Mekadesh – The Lord who sanctifies (Leviticus 20:8)
- Yahweh Raphe – The Lord who heals (Exodus 15:26)
- Elohim – God in three persons (Genesis 1:1)
- El Elohe Israel – The Lord God of Israel (Genesis 33:20)
- Adonai – My Lord (Genesis 15:2)
- El Shaddai – God Almighty (Genesis 17:1)
- El Olam – Eternal God (Genesis 21:33)
- El Gibbor – Mighty God (champion) (Isaiah 9:6)
- El Elyon – God Most High (Genesis 14:18)

Names of Christ from Isaiah 9:6
- Wonderful Counsellor
- Mighty God
- Everlasting Father
- Prince of Peace

Names of the Holy Spirit from Isaiah 11:2
- Spirit of wisdom and of understanding
- Spirit of counsel and might
- Spirit of the knowledge and fear of the Lord

Seven names of Christ from John's gospel
- I am the bread of life (6:35, 51)
- I am the light of the world (8:12)
- I am the gate (10:7, 9)
- I am the good shepherd (10:11, 14)
- I am the resurrection and the life (11:25)
- I am the way, the truth and the life (14:6)
- I am the true vine (15:5)

B *Lectio divina*

Lectio divina is Latin for 'divine reading' and began in early monasteries as a way to 'feast on the word'. The four parts are: taking a bite of the word (*lectio*); chewing on it (*meditatio*); savouring the essence of it (*oratio*); and then digesting and making it part of the body (*contemplatio*). This form of meditative prayer can lead to an increased knowledge of Christ.

- **Prepare: 'Be still, and know that I am God' (Psalm 46:10)**
  Take some time to allow yourself to become quiet and still. As each thought arises, lay it down before God. Lay the coming day's events and your associated thoughts and feelings before God. Invite the Holy Spirit to guide you in this time.

- **Lectio: read**
  A slow and gradual reading of the scriptural passage, perhaps several times. In the traditional Benedictine approach, the passage is slowly read four times, each time with a slightly different focus.

- **Meditatio: reflect**
  Lectio divina is less a practice of reading and analysis than one of listening to the inner message of the scripture, delivered through the Holy Spirit. Between each reading take time to chew it over and ponder a particular word, phrase or theme. Wait and listen.

- **Oratio: respond**
  Continue this conversation with the living Word by praying in response to the scripture, letting our hearts speak directly to God.

- **Contemplatio: rest**
  Let go of your thoughts and meditations and let the word of God dwell in you richly and soak into your core as you behold the Lord. Contemplation is silent prayer that expresses love for God; it is communion, and it transforms us from within.

Blessed Lord, who has caused all holy scriptures to be written for our learning, grant us that we may in such wise hear them, read, mark, learn and inwardly digest them, that by patience, and comfort of thy holy Word, we may embrace and ever hold fast the blessed hope of everlasting life, which thou hast given us in our Saviour Jesus Christ. Amen

Thomas Cranmer[2]

C The Examen

This is a Jesuit practice taught by Ignatius of Loyola in the 16th century. It is otherwise known as a 'rummaging through the day' and is a way to give the day back to the Lord.

- **Prepare** – Take some time to allow yourself to become quiet and still. As each thought arises, lay it down before God. Invite the Holy Spirit to guide you in this time.
- **Replay** – Active remembering. What happened today?
- **Recall** – Pay attention to particularly strong feelings, good or bad.
- **Rejoice** – Where did I feel grace today? Where was God particularly present?
- **Repent** – Where did I feel emotional pain today? Where did I sin?
- **Resolve** – To live differently tomorrow, if need be. And sleep with gratitude.

Search me, God, and know my heart;
    test me and know my anxious thoughts.
See if there is any offensive way in me,
    and lead me in the way everlasting.

PSALM 139:23–24

Notes

Preface

1 Psalm 78:1–7 (MSG)
2 Psalm 78:5–6
3 Dietrich Bonhoeffer, *Letters and Papers from Prison* (Fontana, 1959), p. 150.
4 **lauramthomas.com/2018/03/12/gifts-grandparents-give**

1 Twenty-first century grandparents

1 Jeanne Nagle, *Oprah Winfrey: Profile of a media mogul* (ReadHowYouWant, 2008), p. 5. Oprah's grandmother taught her to read at an early age, using the Bible. She first learned to speak publicly at her grandmother's church.
2 Bernice Neugarten and Karol K. Weinstein, 'The changing American grandparent', *Journal of Marriage and Family*, 26:2 (May 1964), pp. 199–204.
3 'Your grandmother is dead.'
4 Henry Festing Jones (ed.), *The Notebooks of Samuel Butler* (The Floating Press, 2014).
5 Susan Krauss Whitbourne, 'Fulfilment at any age', *Psychology Today*, February 2010.
6 Whitbourne, 'Fulfilment at any age'.
7 Allison Pearson, 'A grandparent's love is forever – it is right that the law should protect it', *The Telegraph*, 8 May 2018.
8 Pearson, 'A grandparent's love is forever'.
9 Pearson, 'A grandparent's love is forever'.
10 See, for example, Hermann Vollmer, 'The grandmother: a problem in child-rearing', *American Journal of Orthopsychiatry*, 7:3 (July 1937); Clifford A. Strauss, 'Grandma made Johnny delinquent', *American Journal of Orthopsychiatry*, 13:2 (April 1943).

11   My mother-in-law, born 1926.
12   My mother, born 1921.
13   Josh Glancy, 'Evolution dictates you tell us a story, Gran!', *The Sunday Times*, 8 April 2018.

2 Memories of the future

1   Igor Stravinsky, *Chronicle of My Life* (Victor Gollancz, 1936).
2   Psalm 68:6
3   Ephesians 1:4–5

3 The art of listening

1   Dietrich Bonhoeffer, *Life Together* (HarperCollins, 1991).
2   Erling Kagge, *Silence: In the age of noise* (Viking, 2017).
3   Michael G. Maudlin, 'Preface' in C.S. Lewis, *A Year with Aslan: Words of spiritual wisdom and reflection from The Chronicles of Narnia* (HarperCollins, 2010).
4   Romans 11:33
5   Psalm 23:4
6   1 Timothy 4:12
7   1 Corinthians 14:3
8   Jeremiah 23:16
9   Psalm 19:1
10   Kagge, *Silence in the Age of Noise*, p. 83.
11   *The Times*, 3 May 2018.

4 This sunrise of wonder

1   Michael Mayne, *This Sunrise of Wonder: Letters to my grandchildren* (DLT, 2008), p. 53.
2   Gerard Manley Hopkins, 'God's Grandeur', quoted in Mayne, *This Sunrise of Wonder*, p. 70.
3   Isaiah 6:3
4   Mayne, *This Sunrise of Wonder*, p. 74.
5   1 John 4:7

6 Colossians 1:15
7 John 10:7, 9
8 John 14:23
9 See Isaiah 43:2.
10 Psalm 31:15
11 John 3:4
12 John 17:3
13 1 John 4:10, 19
14 John 20:18
15 John 21:25
16 Luke 8:43–48
17 See Jeremiah 20:9.
18 Colossians 1:17
19 Quoted in John C. Maxwell, *Developing the Leader within You* (Thomas Nelson, 1993), ch. 3.
20 Proverbs 20:6–7
21 2 Corinthians 2:15
22 Galatians 5:22–23
23 See Mark 1:11; Matthew 25:23.
24 Immaculée Ilibagiza, *Left to Tell: Discovering God amidst the Rwandan genocide* (Hay House, 2006).

5 A grandparent's creed

1 C.S. Lewis, 'Is theology poetry?', lecture to the Oxford Socratic Club, 1944.
2 Mayne, *This Sunrise of Wonder*, p. 71.
3 Genesis 1:31
4 See bibleinoneyear.org/bioy/commentary/2888, 29 April 2018.
5 *Napoleon at St Helena: The journals of General Bertrand January–May 1821* (Doubleday, 1952).
6 Anthony Burgess, 'Review of Kazantzaki's, *The Last Temptation of Christ*', *Yorkshire Post*, March 1961.
7 1 John 4:9
8 Mayne, *This Sunrise of Wonder*, p. 65.
9 See **bartleby.com/357/84.html**.
10 John 3:16 (NIV, MSG)
11 John 15:13
12 2 Corinthians 9:15

13 Colossians 1:15–17
14 Philippians 2:6–8 (MSG)
15 John 14:6
16 Genesis 6:5
17 Jeremiah 17:9
18 Genesis 2:17
19 Genesis 3:5
20 Philippians 4:8
21 Genesis 2:24; Matthew 19:5–6; Ephesians 5:31
22 I also understand the controversial and complex nature of such convictions. I hope this book will lead to good and loving conversations around these tender topics.
23 Genesis 4:7
24 Romans 7:15, 18–19 (MSG)
25 Peter Hitchens, *The Mail on Sunday*, 1 April 2018.
26 C.S. Lewis, *The Lion, The Witch and The Wardrobe* (Fontana, 1950), p. 75.
27 Revelation 21:3–4
28 Hebrews 7:25
29 Genesis 1–2
30 Psalm 139:7
31 Acts 1:5; John 14:26; 2 Thessalonians 2:13; 2 Corinthians 3:18
32 Acts 1:8
33 Acts 2:8–11, 14–41
34 2 Timothy 1:7
35 Galatians 2:20
36 George Frideric Handel, *Messiah*, Part Two, 23, 24.
37 Joel 2:28
38 John 17:11
39 Psalm 139:24
40 John 21:9–13; 20:26
41 1 Corinthians 15:53–54 (MSG)
42 C.S. Lewis, *The Four Loves* (Harper Collins, 1960), p. 168.
43 Timothy Keller, *Hidden Christmas: The surprising truth behind the birth of Christ* (Hodder and Stoughton, 2016), p. 25.

6 Books and the book of books

1   Abridged from Charles Spurgeon, *Speeches by C.H. Spurgeon: At home and abroad* (Passmore and Alabaster, 1878).
2   Quoted by Pope Francis. See Jules Germain, '"The Bible Is an extremely dangerous book," Pope tells young people', *Aleteia*, 17 October 2015, **aleteia.org/2015/10/17/the-bible-is-an-extremely-dangerous-book-pope-tells-young-people**.
3   Psalm 19:1
4   John 5:39
5   See, for example, Amy Orr-Ewing, *Why Trust the Bible?* (IVP, 2006).
6   2 Timothy 3:16
7   2 Peter 1:20–21. We should note that the Bible doesn't avoid the question of false prophecy (see Jeremiah 23:9–40).
8   C.H. Spurgeon, *Morning and Evening Daily Devotional Readings*, 12 October, **morningandevening.org/morning-and-evening-daily-devotional-reading-october-12**.
9   Carl Sagan quoted in Leon Jaroff, 'What's up with the universe?', *Time*, 9 January 1995.
10 Psalm 119:18
11 Psalm 119:24
12 Matthew 10:26
13 Hebrews 4:13
14 Hebrews 4:12
15 Genesis 22:12, 14
16 Genesis 22:5 (italics mine)
17 Mark 15:34
18 Genesis 1:31
19 Genesis 1:3
20 Genesis 1:26
21 Psalm 139:13
22 William N. Blair and Bruce F. Hunt, *The Korean Pentecost* (Banner of Truth, 1977), pp. 27–30.

7 Wonderful and terrible

1   Hebrews 11:9
2   Hebrews 11:1
3   Hebrews 11:13
4   Genesis 13:14-17
5   2 Samuel 12:23
6   1 Samuel 2:21
7   Genesis 13:2
8   Genesis 23:11
9   James 1:14–15
10   Genesis 16:12
11   1 Samuel 23:2
12   Genesis 18:11
13   Exodus 20:16
14   Numbers 32:23
15   Genesis 25:19—33:20
16   Genesis 31:28
17   Genesis 31:35
18   Genesis 28:13–15
19   Genesis 28:10–22; 32:22–32
20   Genesis 33
21   Genesis 37—51
22   Genesis 43:14
23   Genesis 35:11
24   Genesis 46:4
25   Genesis 46:29
26   2 Kings 18—21
27   2 Timothy 1:5; 3:14–15
28   Luke 2:26
29   1 Timothy 5:6, 13; Titus 2:3

8 The body beautiful

1   Dietrich Bonhoeffer, *Letters and Papers from Prison* (Fontana, 1959), p. 166.
2   Ephesians 5:25–27
3   Acts 2:42–47; 4:32–35

4 Matthew 16:18 (ESV)
5 Mark Sayers, *Disappearing Church: From cultural relevance to gospel resilience* (Moody, 2016); Steve Aisthorpe, *The Invisible Church: Learning from the experiences of churchless Christians* (St Andrews, 2016).
6 Compassion UK survey, 2016.
7 Hebrews 10:25
8 John 1:46 (ESV)
9 Quoted by Amy Richter, 'Seeking balance in a frantic world – a Christian approach', speech at NEHM annual conference, 9 May 2013, **episcopalhealthministries.org/files/file/nehm-address-seeking-balance-in-a-frantic-world-a-christian-approach.pdf**.
10 John 10:10
11 Augustine, *Confessions*, 1.1.1
12 Mayne, *This Sunrise of Wonder*, p. 12.
13 **churchofengland.org/prayer-and-worship/join-us-daily-prayer**
14 Matthew 13:19
15 Daniel 6:24
16 Matthew 3:15
17 Bonhoeffer, *Life Together*.

9 Shifting tectonic plates

1 Greg Anderson, 'Effects of earthquakes', lecture notes, **topex.ucsd. edu/es10/es10.1997/lectures/lecture20/secs.with.pics/lecture20. html**.
2 1 Peter 3:15 (MSG)
3 Genesis 1:27
4 John Stott, *Issues Facing Christians Today* (Zondervan, 2011), ch. 12.
5 Ecclesiastes 3:11
6 From a Wikipedia article that has since been updated, but see **en.wikipedia.org/wiki/LGBT**.
7 Genesis 1:31
8 Jo Swinney and Katharine Hill, *Keeping Faith: Being family when belief is in question* (Scripture Union, 2012), pp. 111, 115, 116.
9 *Sunday Telegraph*, May 2018
10 Ephesians 3:18–19

10 Keeping faith when faith is in question

1   Jane Austen, *Northanger Abbey* (1817).
2   A core value of Cruse Bereavement Care.
3   Care for the Family and Hope, *Faith in our Families: A research report*, p. 3, **careforthefamily.org.uk/wp-content/uploads/2014/08/Faith-in-our-Families-Research-booklet-Mar-2018-FINAL.pdf**.
4   The case of Alfie Evans, a 23-month-old boy who died after spending more than a year in hospital, attracted widespread media attention because of a conflict of opinion about the best course of action and treatment. The case of eleven-month-old Charlie Gard in 2017 attracted similar attention for similar reasons.
5   Psalm 71:18
6   Acts 8:26-40
7   Edited from sermon 'Staying Connected', 15 May 2018, **stjamesleith.org.uk**.
8   Romans 14:10, 12–13
9   Romans 15:7
10 Ephesians 4:2

11 A grandparent's prayers

1   E.M. Bounds, *A Treasury of Prayer* (Bethany House, 1961), p. 71.
2   Romans 8:26–27
3   Romans 8:26 (MSG)
4   Psalm 139:2–4
5   Psalm 139:1
6   Jeremiah 20:8–9
7   Jeremiah 6:10
8   1 Samuel 8:3
9   1 Thessalonians 5:17
10 2 Timothy 1:5
11 Katharine Hill, *Left to Their Own Devices: Confident parenting in a world of screens* (Muddy Pearl, 2017).
12 Jeremiah 8:21; 9:1; 8:18
13 Psalm 55:16–17, 22–23
14 See Appendix A.
15 1 John 5:14–15

16 James 4:3
17 James 4:2
18 2 Peter 3:8
19 Luke 18:1
20 Galatians 6:9
21 William J. Bennett, *Tried by Fire: The story of Christianity's first thousand years* Nelson, 2016), p. 208.
22 Psalm 56:8 (NIV and ESV)
23 2 Kings 20:5
24 Psalm 1:3
25 Psalm 131:1
26 See Ephesians 1:3–4
27 See Ephesians 3:18–20
28 1 Samuel 17:47
29 Swinney and Hill, *Keeping Faith*, p. 78.
30 Psalm 38:9
31 Isaiah 55:10–11
32 Matthew 20:16
33 Joel 2:25

12 What about me?

1 C.S. Lewis, *The Four Loves* (Harper Collins, 1960), p. 85.
2 Peter Scazzero, *The Emotionally Healthy Church* (Zondervan, 2010), p. 137.
3 Matthew 4:4
4 See Appendix B – and do it.
5 Genesis 18:17
6 Exodus 33:11
7 John 15:15
8 A retreat is a specific time (anything from a few hours to a month) spent away from one's normal life for the purpose of reconnecting with God through prayer, reading, silence and often an hour's meeting every day. Although monastic communities, such as the Desert Fathers, are as old as Christianity itself, the practice of spending a specific time away with God is a more modern phenomenon, dating from the 1520s and St Ignatius of Loyola's spiritual exercises. With the rediscovery of the contemplative traditions in recent years, retreats have once again become popular

and widely practised. Jesus fasting in the desert for 40 days is used as a biblical justification for retreats.

9   See louvre.fr/en/oeuvre-notices/christ-and-abbot-mena.

10 Isaiah 9:6

11 Mike Mason, *The Mystery of Marriage: Meditations on the miracle* (Multnomah, 2005), pp. 103, 20.

12 Paul Tournier, *Learning to Grow Old* (SCM Press, 2012), p. 44.

13 Tournier, *Learning to Grow Old*, p. 76.

14 See Matthew 6:34

15 Henri Nouwen, *Seeds of Hope* (DLT, 1989), p. 6.

16 Robert Putnam, *Bowling Alone: The collapse and revival of American community* (Simon and Schuster, 2000).

17 Nouwen, *Seeds of Hope*, p. 76.

18 *General Lifestyle Survey 2008* (Office for National Statistics, 2011).

19 See Appendix C – and do it.

20 Lewis, *The Four Loves*

21 Augustine, *Confessions*, 73:3.

22 Proverbs 18:24

23 Lewis, *The Four Loves*, pp. 107–108.

24 Proverbs 17:17

25 Proverbs 15:31–32

26 Proverbs 27:6

27 2 Chronicles 20:7; Isaiah 41:8; James 2:23

28 Matthew 26:50

29 Lewis, *The Four Loves*, p. 147.

30 Proverbs 18:24 (ESV)

31 Henri Nouwen, *Out of Solitude: Three meditations on the Christian life* (Ave Maria Press, 2004).

32 Jean Vanier, *Community and Growth* (Paulist Press, 2004).

33 Psalm 91:1–2, 4

Appendices

1   I heard this from John Wimber, but I no longer have the source of the quote.

2   Book of Common Prayer.

Select bibliography

Jean Vanier, *Community and Growth* (Darton, Longman and Todd, 2006).

Dietrich Bonhoeffer, *Life Together* (HarperCollins, 1991).

Michael Mayne, *This Sunrise of Wonder: Letters to my grandchildren* (Darton, Longman and Todd, 2008)

Paul Brand and Philip Yancey, *Pain: The gift nobody wants* (Diane Publishing, 1999).

C.S. Lewis, *The Four Loves* (Harper Collins, 1960).

C.S. Lewis, *The Problem of Pain* (HarperCollins, 1940)

Jo Swinney and Katharine Hill, *Keeping Faith: Being family when belief is in question* (Scripture Union, 2012)

John Stott, *Issues Facing Christians Today* (Zondervan, 2011).

Mike Mason, *The Mystery of Marriage: Meditations on the miracle* (Multnomah Books, 2005).

Paul Tournier, *Learning to Grow Old* (SCM Press, 2012)

Henri Nouwen, *Seeds of Hope* (Darton, Longman and Todd, 1989)